SYSTEMS OF HIGHER EDUCATION:
FEDERAL REPUBLIC OF GERMANY

Hansgert Peisert
Gerhild Framhein

 International Council for Educational Development

Copyright © 1978 by International Council for Educational Development
ISBN Number: 0-89192-206-7
Printed in the United States of America
Distributed by Interbook Inc., 13 East 16th Street, New York, New York 10003 USA

CONTENTS

FOREWORD

PREFACE

I	**DESCRIPTION OF THE SYSTEM**	1
1	**Design and Function**	3
	Classical Tradition and Present Purposes	3
	Institutional Types and Enrollment	6
	Institutional Governance	18
II	**MANAGEMENT OF THE SYSTEM**	25
2	**Coordinating and Planning Bodies**	29
	Decentralized Reconstruction, 1945–1956	29
	Systemwide Initiatives, 1957–1969	35
	Cooperative Federalism, Since 1969	40
3	**Planning**	49
	Planning System	49
	Plans of the Central Bodies	55
	Data Gathering	63
	Planning Data	67
	Space and Personnel Capacities	74
4	**Administration**	85
	Finance	85
	Admission of Students	92
	Selection of Faculty	98
	Development and Change in Curriculum	101
	Establishment of New Institutions	103

III	**EFFECTIVENESS OF HIGHER EDUCATION**		113
	5 Innovation and Flexibility		117
	Structural Reforms		117
	Innovation in Learning		125
	Reform Under Conditions of Constraint		132
	6 Higher Education and the Social Context		141
	Manpower		141
	Individual Demand and Equality of Opportunity		151
	Research		160
	7 Efficiency		177
	Planning Bodies		177
	Cooperation Between Bund and Länder		183
	Relationship Between Government and Institutions		189

APPENDIX   199

SELECTED BIBLIOGRAPHY   203

LIST OF COUNTRY DIRECTORS   205

FOREWORD

An important and largely unexamined development in higher education is the emergence of systems of institutions, which are planned and managed by advisory, coordinating, or governing bodies poised between institutions and governments. Countries with highly centralized governments now seek to devolve responsibility on such organizations, while in other countries the effort is to move from individual autonomous institutions to more central planning and controls. In both cases, a balance is sought between the values of institutional independence and public responsibility. Problems of organization and procedure are similar but patterns of solution vary widely. The design and management of the systems are, therefore, of universal interest and merit comparative study.

The central issue is easy to state but extremely difficult to answer: How can systems of higher education be designed and managed so as to assure maximum flexibility for institutions with responsible monitoring of the public interest?

Everywhere on the international scene, institutions of higher education are seeing their autonomy challenged—their right to decide their own methods of operation in management, in teaching, and in setting their own goals and purposes. Whether the institutions are public or private, this independence is directly threatened. Public funds and planning call for accountability and service in the national interest as government and society may see it.

The International Council for Educational Development has, for some years, watched this development. It produced what was, to our knowledge, the first collection of essays on the subject in 1972 under the title *Higher Education: From Autonomy to Sys-*

tems. So we welcomed the opportunity provided through a generous grant from the Krupp Foundation of the Federal Republic of Germany to make a three-year comparative analysis of how different countries are adjusting their higher education systems to meet the new demands.

Twelve countries were invited to participate. Guidelines were given for the study with the admonition that they were not to be inflexibly followed: each country needed latitude to explain its own context, development, and unique characteristics. Some problems would be more pertinent to one country than another. Further, we asked for a frank evaluation. Aside from the first section requesting a description of the system with data on institutions, enrollment, and various patterns of governance, the body of each study rests on the informed opinion of leaders in the higher education of the country.

In this respect the study differs from many preceding efforts to draw comparisons based on quantifiable facts. Seldom has that approach yielded more than a collection of data presented in a series of separate descriptions. So we have endeavored to go one step further and provide critical analysis of the issues being faced and the solutions being tried.

The study, in its entirety, comprises: twelve books, one for each country; a volume, crossing national lines, which explores the five major topics selected for analysis—planning, administration, and management; coordination; effectiveness of the system in meeting its social purposes; the effectiveness of the system to change and adjust; and the efficiency of the system—and finally, there is a concluding report.

On a broad scale this study offers a statement about how different countries are dealing with critical problems of educational planning and operations. It speaks to social scientists and public officials who are necessarily concerned with problems of social unrest and cohesion as well as finance and changing priorities. It further holds the prospect of learning from the experience of others. Most educational systems have imported ideas from abroad, or at least they have been stimulated frequently by others to think creatively about their own systems. Also the study provides the means to learn of others' successes as well as difficulties. Finally, there is the responsibility of discovering some general rules of governance that should be studied carefully by all those concerned with macroplanning of higher education.

We urge a careful reading of this study on the Federal Republic of Germany. It will be enlightening to the intracountry audience as a comment on their present situation. For interested parties in other countries, it is a critique that will illuminate their own efforts and stage of development. And those working at the frontier of international comparative studies in higher education will discover, we trust, a valuable piece in an international puzzle.

We are most grateful to Mr. Hansgert Peisert of the University of Konstanz and his colleague, Gerhild Framhein, for this very important report.

February 1978

James A. Perkins
Nell P. Eurich

PREFACE

The German system of higher education, which James B. Conant once called the best system for the nineteenth century, is undergoing profound changes. In recent years, the necessary transition from an elitist to an open system of higher education, which is to serve about one-fourth of the college-age population, has resulted in a complex planning system which is being established in the critical zone delineated by university autonomy, the Länder's* authority, and the federal government.

The following account of past and future developments of the system of higher education in the Federal Republic, or, as some would prefer to call it, in the Länder of the Federal Republic, is part of an international comparison of systems of higher education in twelve countries. In order to assure a comparative evaluation of the individual analyses, the International Council for Educational Development (ICED), as the initiator and coordinator of the study, provided an outline defining the general structure for the presentations.

We have tried to follow the suggested outline rather closely and to present an account that would be informative for German and foreign readers alike. Faced with the plethora of documents and analyses on the various aspects of the Federal Republic's system of higher education, we felt at times, as if we were struggling against a hydra with nine heads, each of which was replaced by two after one was cut off. But we are grateful to ICED for

---

* In the text, the individual states of the Federal Republic of Germany will be called Land (singular) or Länder (plural) since they do not entirely correspond to the "states" of the United States. Also, mostly for the sake of brevity, the Federal Republic of Germany will at times be referred to as the Bund. *(Trans.)*

providing this challenge for, without it, we would not have attempted a comprehensive review of the German system of higher education.

We hope to have given due consideration to the various points of view on this sometimes very controversial subject. We want to express our appreciation for the advice and information received from many parts. We could not have accepted ICED's invitation had it not been for the cooperation of our close colleagues, the availability of research facilities of Center I Educational Research of the University of Konstanz, and the working conditions provided by the European Coordination Center for Research and Documentation in the Social Sciences at Vienna. We would also like to thank Dr. Lucie Karcic for her work in translating the final report.

February 1978   Hansgert Peisert (Konstanz)
                                 Gerhild Framhein (Vienna)

I
DESCRIPTION OF THE SYSTEM

1 DESIGN AND FUNCTION

Classical Tradition and Present Purposes

The German universities have a renowned tradition which goes back to the neohumanist university reforms linked particularly with the name of Wilhelm von Humboldt. When the University of Berlin was founded at the beginning of the nineteenth century, Humboldt formulated those principles which have given the classical German university its specific character and which have had a lingering effect until the present. The essential points were the following: extensive internal autonomy of the state universities; their self-administration through *Ordinarien* (chaired professors heading a department); emphasis on research free of immediate social concerns; and the distinction of a university education from the education in elementary and secondary schools and from professional practice.

Corresponding to this were the principles of "freedom of teaching and learning" for professors and students and of the "unity of research and teaching." The purpose of university instruction and studies was not to transmit knowledge by rote learning, but to acquaint students with research and to allow them to actively participate in it. This principle, formulated as "education through research," became an important didactic tool. It was to guarantee not only a first-rate academic education, but also to train students to think independently and to contribute to the development of those general characteristics that were considered important for the prominent position a university-educated person would occupy both in his profession and in society.[1] When the university system was being reconstructed after World War II, the rebuilding was based on the confident notion that "at its core, the German university is sound" (a phrase that had been coined after World War I). The autonomy of the universities was restored, self-administration carried out by the *Ordinarien* was strengthened, and the generally unstructured process of teaching and research was reintroduced. This system was based on the assumption that the secondary education which students had received in the *Gymnasium* enabled them—largely on their own—to acquire from the university those qualifications necessary for a successful completion of studies.

The goal of the classical university system was to provide an academic education to a small elite. In the past two decades, however, the Federal Republic's system of higher education has been expanded to serve a larger proportion of the population. This has not only resulted in expansion and reform of the traditional university system but in restructuring the tertiary education sector altogether. This development has been marked —from an institutional point of view—by changing the legal status and instructional forms of various vocational institutions to resemble universities. These institutions have been combined with the universities into a new system of higher education.

The official documents preparing and accompanying the structural changes emphasize that the goal of the restructuring of higher education is to overcome the elitist university system and to offer higher education that is demand-oriented.[2]

> The educational policy of a democratic society must be based on the principle of the civil right to education. Hence, the reform of higher education must lead to a university structure that gives every citizen the opportunity to obtain an education and an occupation in line with his abilities, regardless of the income and educational background of his parents.

The tasks of the entire system of higher education have been defined in the Frame Law for Higher Education (*Hochschulrahmengesetz*—HRG) passed in 1976. Stressing "research" and "teaching and studies," the tasks as stated tie in with the classic functions of the universities; these have been supplemented by an explicit connection between academic training and professional practice. As the frame law states:

> *Tasks of Higher Education:* It is the function of the institutions of higher education to serve and develop sciences* and arts through research, teaching, and studies. The institutions prepare the students for professions that either demand the application of scientific knowledge and scientific methods, or the capability for artistic creation. (HRG Art. 2.1).
>
> *Purpose of Studies:* Teaching and studies are to prepare the student for a professional field; in reference to the respective courses of study they are to transmit the necessary knowledge, proficiency, and methods in such a way as to enable the student to carry out scientific or artistic work in a profession and to act responsibly in a liberal, democratic, social, and constitutional state (Art. 7).
>
> *Research Tasks:* The function of research in higher education is to obtain scientific knowledge and to provide for the scientific foundation and advancement of teaching and studies. All areas of science, as well as the practical application of scientific knowledge including the consequences that may follow its application, can be the subject of research at institutions of higher education, depending on the particular nature of an individual institution (Art. 22).

Within this legal framework, there is no longer any insistence upon the unity of research and teaching in the strict, classical sense. The ratio between research, teaching, and studies remains open. It is only defined insofar as the institutions, in cooperation with government agencies, are given the permanent task to develop and adjust the contents and form of studies to new developments in science and art and also to the changing needs of the professional world.[3]

---

* The German term *'Wissenschaft'* embraces the arts and the various branches of science—medical, technical, and so on. In its wider meaning, it also covers all areas of learning, including research, teaching, and studies. In this paper the term will be translated simply as "science." (*Trans.*)

Under the 1976 law, the freedom of teaching and learning, characteristic of German universities, has been limited somewhat: the length of time a student should spend in a given course of study is to be defined and differentiated; study regulations are to be introduced that indicate courses and achievements a student must accomplish in order to complete his studies successfully. Within these limits, students are still free to change institutions, to choose among courses, and to follow special interests in their studies according to their own choice.[4] The euphoria, with which even in post-war times the principle of "education through research" was emphasized as being the real aim of higher education has yielded to a certain sobriety.

There is no doubt, however, that an academic course of study is still expected to influence significantly the general personal development of the students, particularly their rational and critical faculties and their ability to act responsibly. While in the United States such personal educational goals are pursued through extensive liberal arts programs, the institutions of higher education in the Federal Republic are still confident that the pursuit of knowledge in specific scientific areas has a positive formative effect upon the student. The emphasis on practice-orientation in the 1976 regulations indicates, however, that research, teaching, and studies are not to be confined to academic ivory towers and should instead be aimed more at professional and social demands.

Institutional Types and Enrollment

After World War II, the system of higher education reverted to the meager remnants of the German university system of the Weimar Era. The fundamental hostility of the Third Reich toward science had resulted in a considerable reduction of faculty and students at the universities. In the winter semester 1932/33, the last semester before the national-socialist seizure of power, 121,000 students were still enrolled at the German universities.

Five years later, in the winter semester 1938/39 shortly before World War II, the number of students had dwindled by more than half—to 56,000. Of the twenty-four universities and fourteen technical universities, sixteen universities and nine technical universities were located in that part of Germany which was to become the Federal Republic; the German Democratic Republic had six universities and three technical universities, while two universities and two technical universities were located on territory that today is part of Poland.

In contrast to the totalitarian centralist cultural administration of the Third Reich, the Federal Republic reestablished the cultural-federalistic authority of the Länder. Hence, the rebuilding of the system of higher education was mainly the responsibility of the ministries of culture in the eleven Länder of the Federal Republic. Private institutions have never played a significant role in German higher education.

Initially, the traditional universities and technical universities formed the nucleus of the postwar system of higher education. They have doubled in number since 1945. Since two-thirds of all students attend the universities and technical universities, these institutions are still, as far as numbers are concerned, the most important sector in the system of higher education. The quantitatively less significant theological seminaries (now enrolling 0.2 percent of all students) and the art academies have always been included in this sector. This system of higher education has gradually been extended to include, first, the teachers colleges, and since the beginning of the seventies, the *Fachhochschulen* and the new comprehensive institutions of higher education. The present system of higher education, therefore, is composed of the following six types of institutions: universities (including technical universities); teachers colleges; theological seminaries; art academies; *Fachhochschulen;* and comprehensive institutions of higher education.

Studies at universities and university-type institutions (teachers colleges and theological seminaries) and in university-type courses at comprehensive institutions require the "maturity" certificate. Primarily, this is the general university qualification (*Abitur*) granted by the *Gymnasium* after thirteen years of schooling. In addition, there are special-area *Gymnasien* which grant a discipline-oriented university qualification that entitles the student only to enter specific programs of study. The certificate of qualification for studies at *Fachhochschulen* is acquired, as a rule, by passing the final examination of a special area or vocational secondary school after twelve years of schooling. In some Länder, students are allowed to enter a *Fachhochschule* upon completion of the twelfth grade at a *Gymnasium*. Entrance requirements for art academies vary. The general trend is, however, to require the *Abitur*. All students who intend to enter an art academy must give proof of specific artistic talents (entrance examination). Chart I schematically illustrates the progression from the primary and secondary levels to the tertiary level.

Institutions

Universities

With respect to their historical development, there are three different types of universities. First, there are the "old" universities—for example, Heidelberg, Freiburg, and Tübingen—some of which date back to the Middle Ages. Their programs of study were developed from the classical faculties of medicine, law, theology, and philosophy. The natural, economic, and social sciences were added later as independent faculties.

A second type is comprised of those institutions which were established to offer higher education in special areas. Among these are primarily the technical universities, as well as schools of medicine and economics. Some of these institutions continue to exist as special institutions with university status; others have been expanded into universities by adding more departments.

A third type comprises the new universities created since the sixties. These new institutions were intended to increase the capacity and improve the regional distribution of higher education facilities. Also, their creation was linked with the aim of introducing the structural reform of the traditional universities

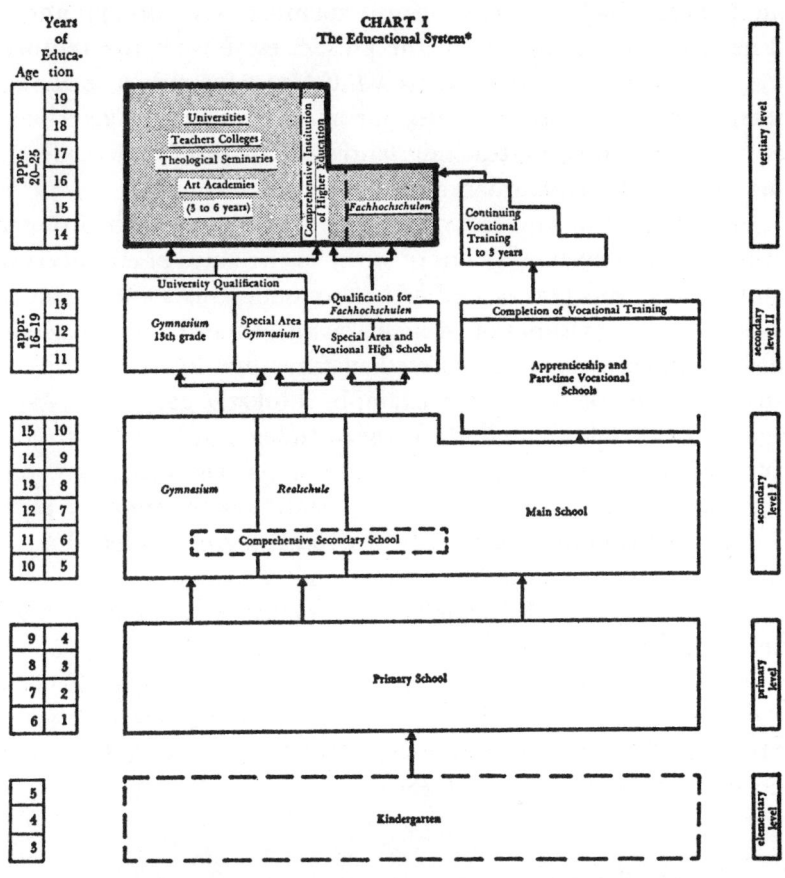

CHART I
The Educational System*

*The structural chart does not indicate quantitative proportions of the individual institutions. The arrows indicate the most common transitions.

(for instance, with regard to the structure of programs and their internal organization).

Research and the privilege of administering examinations together with the awarding of degrees such as the diploma, master's, and doctorate degrees as well as granting the qualification for university teaching (*Habilitation*) belong to the traditional and legally established fundamental rights of the universities.[5] Proof of successful completion of studies is demonstrated either with a state-board examination or with an academic-university examination (diploma, master's, doctorate). State-board examinations are administered by state boards of examiners to which, as a rule, faculty members are also appointed. The state, in the interest of the public, establishes the requirements for the state-board exams, which exist for only a relatively small number of professions: medicine (including veterinary and dental medicine), teaching (currently in forty-four academic disciplines), law, pharmaceutics, and food chemistry.

With regard to university examinations, exams for a diploma apply to sixty-seven programs of study in the fields of engineering and natural sciences, as well as in economic and social sciences. The master's examination, which was introduced for disciplines in the humanities, is now offered in fifty-nine different subjects. In a number of fields—for example, biology, geography, pedagogics, psychology, and sociology—students may take an examination for both a diploma and a master's degree and, depending upon their professional goal, a state examination as well. Today, a doctorate is generally a second degree preceded by a state, diploma, or master's examination.

Of the forty-nine universities now in existence, about one-half are large universities that each enrolled between 10,000 to 35,000 students in summer 1977. The University of Munich (35,000), the Free University of Berlin (33,000), and the universities of Münster (29,000) and Hamburg (27,000) are the four largest universities in the Federal Republic.

Teachers Colleges

The predecessors of the teachers colleges were the pedagogic institutes. There were eighty such institutes in the beginning of the 1950s; their number had risen to more than one-hundred by the end of the sixties. In the early 1970s, thirty of the institutes became independent teachers colleges with university-type status; others were incorporated into existing universities.

The main purpose of the teachers colleges is the education of teachers for primary and lower level secondary schools. At the end of their studies, these students have to pass a state-board examination. In conjunction with their research tasks in educational science and teaching methodology, many teachers colleges are entitled to grant diplomas and doctoral degrees (doctor of philosophy or doctor of educational science). As a rule, student enrollment at the teachers colleges runs between 1,000 and 3,000. The largest teachers colleges are in Berlin and in Münster, with more than 5,000 students each.

Theological Seminaries

Theological seminaries are either church or government institutions that exist outside the theology faculties at universities. In general, these seminaries confer doctor of theology degrees. In recent years, a number of them have been incorporated into the newly founded universities or comprehensive institutions of higher education. Today, eleven independent theological seminaries are still in existence. Altogether, they only have a little over 2,000 students. Within the educational system, their role is, therefore, not very significant.

Art Academies

Among these institutions, there are twenty-six state academies for fine arts, design, dramatic arts, music, film, and television. They prepare the students for a career in the arts. The final degree is either given by the state or by the academy itself. Art academies also educate teachers of art and music for the *Gymnasium* and, in some cases, for lower-level secondary schools. Art academies are mostly smaller institutions; at the moment, only two of them have more than 1,000 students.

Fachhochschulen

Fachhochschulen were established in 1970–71 on the basis of a 1968 agreement between the Länder. The former engineering schools and other advanced vocational schools (e.g. for commerce or for social work), which used to belong to the secondary level of vocational education, have been merged into the *Fachhochschulen*. Next to the universities, the *Fachhochschulen* are today the most important sector of higher education as far as student enrollment is concerned. The numbers of students at these institutions make up almost 20 percent of the entire student population, and they enroll more than 25 percent of all entering students. In contrast to the universities, teachers colleges, and art academies, some *Fachhochschulen* are run as private institutions, mostly by the church; student enrollment at the latter, however, is less than 10 percent of the entire student enrollment at *Fachhochschulen*.

The curricula at *Fachhochschulen* differ from those at the universities. *Fachhochschulen* are more practice-oriented; study periods are shorter (generally three years), and students devote a greater part of their studies to practical vocational training. After completion of their programs, students take a state examination. Graduation from *Fachhochschule* entitles the student to enter a university. Half of the more than 100 *Fachhochschulen* have less than 1,000 students; the four largest have between 4,000 and 8,000 students.

Comprehensive Institutions
of Higher Education

The new type of comprehensive institution of higher education includes university-type programs, programs of *Fachhochschulen*, and, in some cases, those of art academies which are completed with their respective examinations. After completion of university-type programs of study, the doctoral degree may be conferred. The programs at the comprehensive institutions may be integrated (short- and long-term studies) or separated according to the component institutional types (cooperative comprehensive institution).

Since 1970, eleven comprehensive institutions of higher education have been created in North Rhine Westphalia, Hesse, and Bavaria, partly by combining already existing institutions. One, founded by North Rhine Westphalia in 1974, is also the first extension university in the Federal Republic. Another comprehensive institution is the military academy in Munich. (The military academy in Hamburg is listed among the institutions of university status.)

According to the Frame Law for Higher Education, the system of higher education in the Federal Republic is to be reorganized. The objective is to expand or mold the various types of tertiary institutions into comprehensive institutions, or to guarantee concerted cooperation among the various types of tertiary institutions through joint coordinating boards. (For details on this point, see Chapter 5.)

Table 1 illustrates the proliferation of the six types of tertiary institutions since 1950.[6] The present terminology was also used for the previous structure. The reason for the diminishing number of teachers colleges between 1960 and 1970 lies in their transformation into university-type institutions. In this process, some of the earlier institutions were combined or integrated into the universities. Since there are no precise figures for the schools that were the forerunners of the *Fachhochschulen,* we have omitted this item for 1950 and 1960.

Enrollment

Table 2 shows enrollment figures in the Federal Republic since 1950.[7] In this case, we have reconstructed enrollment numbers for those institutions which formerly were not part of the system of higher education. For the schools that preceded the *Fachhochschulen,* these figures can only be approximated.[8]

If one includes all the types of institutions that are part of the present system of higher education, student numbers increased from approximately 172,000 in 1950 to 837,000 in 1975. In the winter semester of 1977–78, enrollment figures rose to 914,000.

TABLE 1
Institutions of the System of Higher Education, 1950–75

Type of Institution	1950	1960	1970	1975
Universities (including technical universities and special universities)	31	33	40	49
Comprehensive Institutions	—	—	—	11
Teachers Colleges	78	77	32	33
Theological Seminaries	16	17	14	11
Art Academies	18	25	27	26
Fachhochschulen (since 1970)	—	—	98	136
Total	143	152	211	266

TABLE 2
Student Enrollment Figures, 1950–77*

Type of Institution	1950	1960	1970	1975	1977
Universities (including technical universities and special universities)	112,000	217,000	350,000	553,000	606,000
Comprehensive Institutions	—	—	—	42,000	56,000
Teachers Colleges	ca. 10,000	33,000	59,000	79,000	69,000
Theological Seminaries	5,000	3,000	2,000	2,000	2,000
Art Academies	5,000	8,000	11,000	15,000	15,000
Fachhochschulen	ca. 40,000	ca. 68,000	ca. 112,000	146,000	165,000
Total	ca. 172,000	ca. 329,000	ca. 534,000	837,000	914,000
1950 = 100%	100%	191%	311%	486%	531%

* German and foreign students; the figures are those of the winter semesters.

In the sixties, about 7 percent of these students were foreigners; that number has decreased since 1970 to about 6 percent.

This means that student enrollment has increased by more than five times since 1950. At the same time, the proportion of students in the population of the same age group (eighteen to twenty-four years old) increased from 3.5 percent to 14 percent between 1950 and 1975.[9] The proportion of beginning students in the eighteen to twenty-year old population rose during that same period from approximately 6 percent to almost 20 percent.[10] It should be emphasized that student numbers have increased steadily since 1950, and continued to climb rapidly after 1970. This is in contrast to recent trends in other comparable countries where high expansion rates have slowed down during recent years.[11]

Diagram A illustrates the development of student enrollment figures.[12] The dark part represents the traditional university sector and the lighter parts the development of the other institutions which mostly have only later been integrated into the tertiary sector. For 1977, the proportion of students in the different institutional types is indicated.

A division of university students, who constitute about two-thirds of the entire student population, by areas of study presents the following picture:[13] languages and humanities (including theology and athletics with 1.8 percent each)—30 percent; law, economics, and social sciences—23.5 percent; mathematics and natural sciences—20.5 percent; engineering—12.4 percent; medicine—9 percent; arts—2.3 percent; agriculture and nutritional science—2.2 percent. Of the students at *Fachhochschulen*— almost one-fifth of the entire student population—50 percent are in engineering and one-third in economic and social sciences.

Location of Institutions

Institutions of higher education have become more evenly distributed as a result of the creation of many new institutions. As Map 1 indicates, the "Middle West" of the Federal Republic, along the axis Bochum-Frankfurt-Stuttgart, has a dense and regionally well-distributed net of universities, while the North and Southeast show more empty space. For *Fachhochschulen* the situation is similar. Due to their specialization, regional facilities in this sector are, however, more unevenly distributed than the map indicates.

In general, the German system of higher education does not have the Anglo-Saxon type of campus university where students

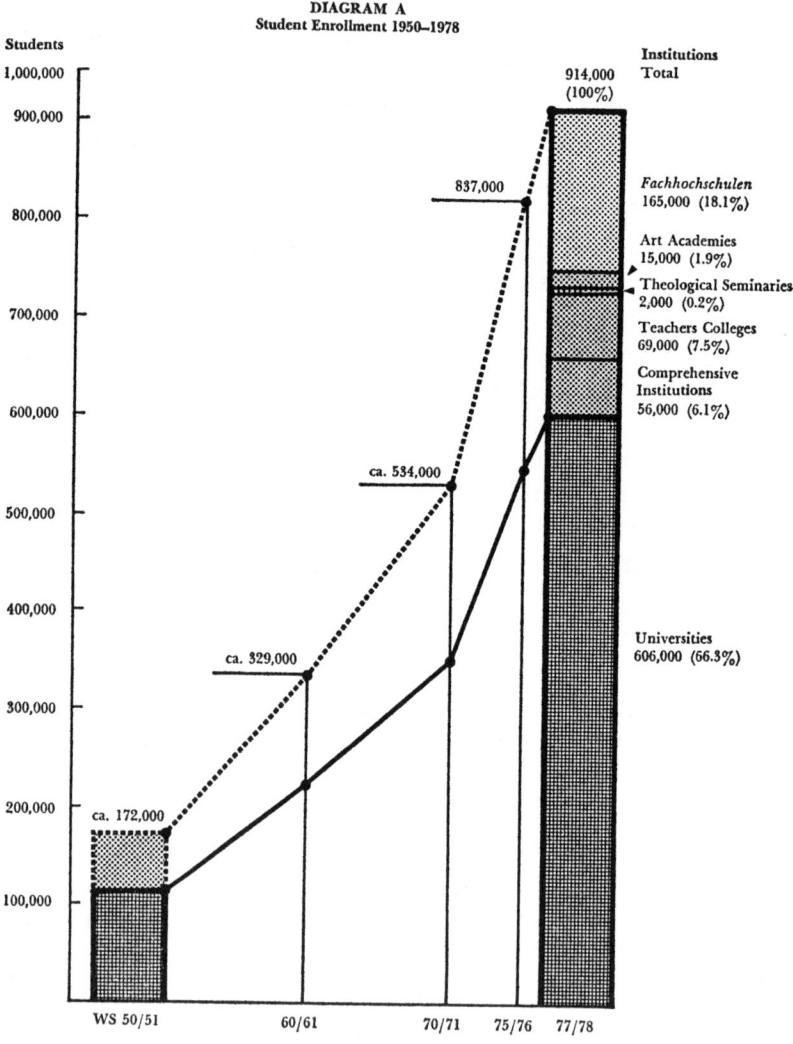

DIAGRAM A
Student Enrollment 1950–1978

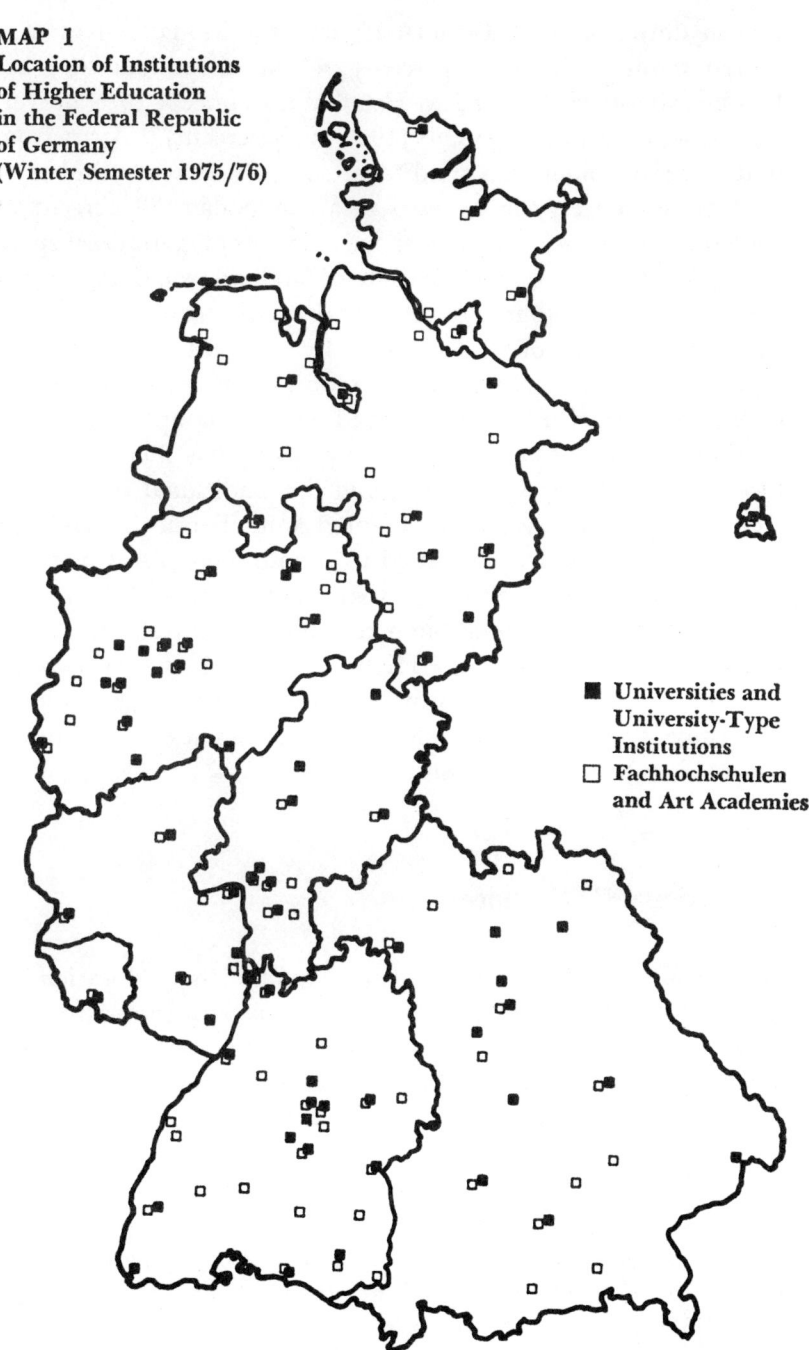

MAP 1
Location of Institutions of Higher Education in the Federal Republic of Germany
(Winter Semester 1975/76)

■ Universities and University-Type Institutions
□ Fachhochschulen and Art Academies

live in dormitories. A German student traditionally lives in a rented room (1956 = 52 percent), which in student lore has become almost as glorified as Humboldt's concept of a university, or with his or her parents (1956 = 33 percent).[14] Apart from that, the government has tried to provide a sufficient number of student residences; the target is to accommodate 30 percent of students.[15] However, in spite of the increase of dormitory space to 90,150 in 1975, only 11 percent of students could be housed because of the rapid growth of student numbers. In the past few years, the number of students who live in rented rooms or at home has decreased (1976: rented rooms = 18 percent; at home = 21 percent). On the other hand, living in apartments (30 percent) or sharing apartments (18 percent) has increased.[16] In this context, an important change in the traditional life-style of German students should be pointed out. Formerly, German students were mobile. They used to choose their places of study independent of the residence of their parents, and in the course of their studies they would often transfer several times from one university to another. They might also spend one or two semesters at a foreign university. Now, this pattern has changed. The present generation of students tends to stay at one institution and as close to home as possible.

Institutional Governance

With a few exceptions, the institutions of higher education in the Federal Republic are public institutions with the traditional right to self-governance. In the postwar period, relations between government and institutions could be characterized as rather distant. Until the end of the sixties there were hardly any legal prescriptions regulating the internal organization of the universities. Government action was largely limited to providing and increasing material resources. Universities were anxious to reestablish their autonomy; their constitutions were based on the principles of academic self-administration established in the nineteenth century.

The most important basic unit of self-administration was the university chair, generally associated with an institute or seminar. In the realm of his unit, the *Ordinarius* (chaired professor) was virtually free to make his own decisions with regard to research and instruction, personnel and budgetary matters. The faculties, as the assembly of *Ordinarien,* were responsible for the broader questions of research and teaching. They had the right to confer doctoral degrees as well as those degrees that entitle a person to teach at a university *(Habilitation).* They also had the right to suggest candidates for appointments. The traditional universities generally had faculties of theology, philosophy, law, medicine, natural sciences, and economics.

The senates, as the universities' central bodies of coordination and academic administration, were composed of representatives of the faculties. These representatives changed every year. The rector, generally elected for a one-year term from the *Ordinarien* of the various faculties, presided over the university as *primus inter pares.* Independent of academic self-administration, the university household was administered by an administrative civil servant appointed by the respective Ministry of Culture.

Because of the prominent position of power occupied by the *Ordinarien,* the German university was characterized as an *Ordinarienuniversität.* Until the middle of the sixties, the remaining members of the university—non-chaired professors, subprofessorial academic staff, students and nonacademic personnel—were mostly excluded from decision-making processes, even though they were occasionally allowed to be represented in the committees of the *Ordinarien.*

The method of governing a university by chaired professors proved to be ineffective when the expansion of institutions of higher education and the development of sciences transformed the universities into large-scale enterprises. Due to the growth and also as a consequence of the student protest movement in the 1960s, conditions at the universities sometimes became so chaotic that the government was provoked to interfere more and more. In this process, the old structure of self-administration became the central target for reforms, an endeavor in which all groups within the universities, their national associations, and finally even the political parties, the parliaments, and the governments participated.

The main issues in the reform were: to organize the institutions into clearly surveyable units according to the Anglo-Saxon model of a departmental structure; to strengthen the central administration; to make it "professional" by appointing a president or rector for a longer term in office; and to make the decision-making process more democratic by giving all groups within the university voting power in university committees.

Initially, the debate on codetermination centered on the problem of involvement of non-chaired professors, subprofessorial staff (mainly the assistants or the so-called middle level), and students in the decision-making process. Later the nonacademic employees of the university, from the superintendent of building to the library employees, were brought in as a fourth group to be involved in the decision-making process. This resulted in the coining of the term "group university," and the question of "parities"—one-third or one-quarter parity—in connection with voting procedures became a major subject of controversy in university politics.

Toward the end of the sixties the individual Länder prepared the first university laws which stipulated that universities were to reorganize their governance structure. As far as composition and participation of the various groups in the self-administration of the universities were concerned, state laws varied considerably. The "University Verdict" of the Federal Constitutional Court of 1973 provided basic guidelines for the state legislatures. According to these guidelines, the professorial groups are to hold the absolute majority in university committees deciding on issues that are of immediate relevance for research and teaching, and to the appointment of new faculty members.[17]

The reform of university governance is still in a state of flux. At present, the Länder laws for higher education which form the legal framework for the constitutions of universities are adapted to the regulations of the federal Frame Law for Higher Education. This allows us to make a rough projection of the future structure of university constitutions. In the Frame Law for Higher Education, the principle of the group university is confirmed. The members of an institution of higher education are divided into four groups: professors (chaired and non-chaired); students; subprofessorial and artistic staff; and other staff.

All of these groups must be represented in the departmental council and in the two central committees of the institutions. Any determination of voting strength must take into consideration the verdict of the Federal Constitutional Court.

The basic organizational units of the institutions are departments headed by a departmental council which is chaired by a professor. Departments either consist of the members of one large academic field or of several smaller, related fields. Hence, the department replaces the former, smaller unit of a chair or institute and the usually larger unit of the former faculties. When the new structure cannot sufficiently carry out the coordinating function that was performed by the former faculties, it is possible to form joint committees that deal with certain common matters (examination regulations, appointments, and so on).

The institution is to have a full-time head (president or rector) who will be in office for at least four years; this function may also be carried out by an elected executive committee, but one of its members must be a full-time member.

Central tasks are to be dealt with by two academic committees. One of them (council, convention, large senate) is the "parliament" of the institution. Its most important duties are the election of the head of the university and decision making pertaining to the constitution of the university. The second committee (senate) is responsible for current operations of the institution. Its most important tasks relate to decision making on development and budgetary planning of the institution, the number of new students to be admitted, the organization of departments and scientific facilities, basic questions of research and academic or artistic succession, and regulations for examinations as well as suggestions for the appointment of professors.

In contrast to the former dual university constitution, which drew a clear line between the academic and budgetary administration, the Frame Law for Higher Education prescribes a unified administration. This means that the chancellor takes care of administrative matters of the institution as a whole and also participates in the administration of departmental matters and central facilities; his special responsibility is the budget. His function has changed from that of curator as the local representative of the state Ministry of Culture to that of a member of the individual institution which he represents vis-á-vis the Ministry of Culture, within the framework of legal regulations.

The laws governing the system of higher education that have been passed in rapid succession by the Bund and the Länder in the past ten years indicate that the era of "splendid isolation" for the universities has come to an end. In the following sections we shall describe the ways in which the general problems of the system are handled, as well as the coordinating and planning committees that have been formed to deal with these questions.

FOOTNOTES

1. For a comprehensive discussion and documentation of the German university tradition and problematic issues relating to reforms since 1945, cf. Helmut Schelsky, *Einsamkeit und Freiheit,* Idee und Gestalt der deutschen Universität und ihrer Reformen (Hamburg: Rowoldt, 1963); Wolfgang Nitsch, U. Gerhardt, C. Offe, U. K. Preuss, *Hochschule in der Demokratie,* Kritische Beiträge zur Erbschaft und Reform der deutschen Universität (Neuwied: Luchterhand, 1965).
2. Federal Ministry of Education and Science, *Regierungsentwurf eines Hochschulrahmengesetzes,* Bonn, August 29, 1973, p. 3.
3. Cf. Frame Law for Higher Education, Art. 8.
4. Cf. *ibid.,* Arts. 3 and 11.
5. The description of the individual types of institutions of higher education follows in general the official description by the secretariat of the Conference of Ministers of Culture (KMK): The Educational System in the Federal Republic of Germany—Responsibilities, Structure, Educational Programs. Draft of January, 1977.
6. Figures for 1950–70: Statistical Yearbooks for the Federal Republic of Germany; *Fachhochschulen* 1970: German Educational Council, *Gutachten und Materialien zur Fachhochschule,* Gutachten und Studien der Bildungskommission 10 (Stuttgart: Klett, 1974); p. 144. Figures for 1975: Federal Office of Statistics, Studenten an Hochschulen WS 1975/

76 (Series 11, No. 4.1). The departments of teachers colleges and *Fachhochschulen* that are in different locations were counted separately.
7. Figures for 1950–70: Statistical Yearbooks for the Federal Republic of Germany; for *Fachhochschulen* (or their predecessors) 1950–70: Estimates by D. Goldschmidt based on unpublished documents of the Federal Office for Statistics; cf. Dietrich Goldschmidt, "Country Profile: Autonomy and Accountability in the Federal Republic of Germany" (Berlin: 1974) mimeo. Figures for 1975: Federal Office for Statistics, Studenten an Hochschulen SS 1977, Preliminary Report (Series 11, No. 4.1). Figures for 1977: Communication from the Federal Office for Statistics.
8. Most statistics only list the student numbers of the former engineering schools. Following Goldschmidt's estimate we have tried to include also those students of the other advanced vocational schools that have become part of the present system of higher education since 1970.
9. Figures based on Table 2 and data of the Statistical Yearbooks about the 18- to 24-year old population.
10. Cf. Science Council, *Empfehlungen zu Umfang und Struktur des Tertiären Bereiches* (Cologne: 1976), p. 10.
11. Cf. Ignace Hecquet, Ch. Vernier, L. Cerych, *Recent Student Flows in Higher Education* (International Council for Educational Development: New York, 1976) mimeo.
12. For these data cf. footnote 7.
13. Figures for winter semester 1975/76. Calculations based on the Federal Office for Statistics, Studenten an Hochschulen WS 1975/76 (Series 11, No. 4.1).
14. Cf. Gerhard Kath, *Das soziale Bild der deutschen Studentenschaft in Westdeutschland und Berlin*—SS 1956 (Bonn: 1957), p. 73.
15. Cf. Federal Ministry of Education and Science, *Bildungsbericht 70* (Bonn: 1977), p. 108.
16. Cf. Deutsches Studentenwerk, *Vorauswertung zur 8. Sozialerhebung— SS 1976* (Bonn: 1977) mimeo, p. 17.
17. Verdict of the Federal Constitutional Court of May 29, 1973, regarding the preliminary regulation of Lower Saxony. Cf. on this point, Ulrich Karpen, Franz-Ludwig Knemeyer, *Verfassungsprobleme des Hochschulwesens* (Paderborn: Ferdinand Schöningh, 1976).

II
MANAGEMENT OF THE SYSTEM

INTRODUCTION

After World War II, the German system of higher education was reconstructed according to a politico-cultural concept that had as its central maxim a turning away from the centralized structure of the previous National-Socialist cultural policy and the renewal of a decentralized system. Hence, the revision of the system of higher education in the Federal Republic of Germany was essentially determined by factors that guaranteed autonomy to the Länder in their cultural affairs and to the institutions of higher education. Today, the idea of a system of dual (Länder-institutional) decentralization is still basic. The question is: how can the ubiquitous problems of growth which confront the system of higher education be solved by a decentralized government system. The need for centralized planning, decision-making, and coordination is rarely questioned: this need, however, must of necessity conflict with a decentralized system.

The increasing financial involvement of the federal government to support science and institutions of higher learning has accelerated this development. It has resulted in a creeping tendency toward centralization and an actual participation in the official domain of the Länder. Moreover, we must bear in mind that the growth of institutions of higher learning requires a transition from the classical academic self-determination of the traditional university system, whose administrative dilettantism had an almost Spitzweg-like* quality, to the demanding, computer-run, systemwide planning of the present mammoth enterprise. This transition is to take place in the realm of detached

---

* Spitzweg was a German painter of the nineteenth century known for his insular, yet humorous subjects. (*Trans.*)

academics who are on principle disinclined toward planning; hence, the infrastructure for planning and coordination beyond regional borders virtually has to be developed anew.

In the following three chapters we shall demonstrate the gradual establishment of nationwide, central committees in the decentralized system of higher education since 1945, and examine how the functions of these committees changed from reactive coordination to planning and decision making (see Chapter 2). Subsequently, we shall describe the planning and decision-making system as it is now being developed, as well as its procedures and projections for further development of the system (see Chapter 3). Finally, we shall deal with some aspects of administration in higher education (see Chapter 4).

2 COORDINATING AND PLANNING BODIES

Decentralized Reconstruction, 1945–1956

The creation of a federation of states of the Federal Republic of Germany was a conscious revival of the traditions of the Weimar Constitution and as such a conscious reaction to the degradation of the centralized state by the National-Socialists from 1933 to 1945. Thus, the federalist principle also had a "moral" quality, an important factor for the evolving national consciousness of the new republic. Because of this specific historical background, and because of the fact that in the course of the twentieth century the states have been forced to yield more and more to a centralized authority on the federal level, the domain of culture has become the prominent focus of federalism. This is supported by the conviction that cultural federalism is specifically suited to promote democratic values. This refers in particular to the preservation of historical and regional cultural diversity, positive competition of cultural policy between the Länder, safeguarding against ideological onesidedness, and a closer relation to grass root concerns.

Thus, the experience with the dictatorship of the centralized state and the confidence in the positive values of cultural federalism help to explain the emphatic insistence of the Länder on cultural autonomy and their sensitive reaction toward centralizing tendencies.

The Basic Law of 1949 granted the Länder general autonomy

for all state affairs (Art. 30, Basic Law), in particular in the cultural domain. In this domain, only minimal powers were given to the federal state:

- the legislative authority of the federal government to promote *scientific research* (Art. 74, p. 13, Basic Law);
- the legislative framework for general jurisdiction of the *press and motion picture industry* (Art. 75, p. 2, Basic Law);
- cultural *relations with foreign nations* (Art. 32, p. 1, Basic Law).

The principle of cultural federalism was limited however by another constitutional norm referring to the preservation of uniform living conditions in all parts of the republic (Art. 72.3, Basic Law). The compatibility of these conflicting principles would later become the fundamental dilemma in the development of cultural federalism.

Following the principle of cultural federalism, the education sector was revived after the war detached from any interference of the Bund. Insofar as systemwide harmonization was desirable, this was carried out solely on the Länder level, among the ministers of culture, and for higher education also on the institutional level, among the university rectors.

Because of their common interest, the ministers of education of the German Länder convened in the beginning of 1948 in Stuttgart-Hohenheim for their first Conference of German Ministers of Education. At their second meeting—after the beginning of the Berlin blockade and therefore now without their colleagues from the Länder of the Soviet-occupied zone—they decided to create a Permanent Conference of the Ministers of Culture of the States of the Federal Republic of Germany (Ständige Konferenz der Kultusminister der Länder in der Bundesrepublik Deutschland—KMK). The ministers of culture of the eleven Länder are members of this conference.[1] Every Land has one vote, and decisions have to be unanimous. Such unanimous decisions, however, are merely suggestions submitted to the Länder who can decide independently on matters of educational policy.

The establishment of the KMK did not originate from a desire for a central planning panel; rather, it was created because the ministers of culture of the Länder wanted a forum for communication and, also, an organ that would represent their interests vis-á-vis the federal government. The rules of procedure state that the KMK is to deal with "politico-cultural matters of national significance, with the objective of reaching a consensus and of advocating common interests."[2]

As early as 1948 the KMK formed the committee on higher education as a standing committee. The traditional uniformity of German universities facilitated coordination. Since 1955, efforts have been directed toward establishing unified guidelines for examinations. Coordination became more important as a result of the growing number of students and the formation of national planning committees. During the first phase, the KMK saw its main problem to be, above all, the heterogeneity of the primary and secondary school system, a result of the fact that the Länder had a history of autonomous statehood. This heterogeneity—considered by some to be "educational chaos"—was generally brought under control by the unifying measures of the Düsseldorf Agreement of 1955.

Within a year after the inception of the KMK, the parliamentary members of the Free Democratic Party (FDP)—the party which in later decades was occasionally to entertain the idea of forming a federal ministry of culture—moved to create a parliamentary committee for cultural policy. The move received a majority vote, against the opposition of the Bavarian Party (BP) and the Christian Social Union (CSU). The diverging educational practices on the primary and secondary levels in the Länder and the resulting restrictions on transferring (and the subsequent restriction on the freedom to move within the country), as well as the absence of a parliamentary body to represent the cultural interests of the Federal Republic on the international level, were the reasons for the vote.

The reaction of the ministers of culture of the Länder to this parliamentary action was expressed very distinctly three weeks later (October 19, 1949) in the Bernkastel Resolution and is still prominently quoted in the KMK handbook. In this resolution the KMK expresses its conviction that:[3]

> the totalitarian and centralistic cultural policy of recent history may partly be held responsible for the ominous confusion and enslaving of the mind, and for the susceptibility of many Germans to amorality. [The KMK] therefore feels bound to the principles of regional and historically grown autonomy, and of diversity of social conditions, as guarantors for the spiritual recovery of the German people and for the organic development of a culture supported by the people themselves . . . It will be the objective of the Permanent Conference of Ministers of Culture to maintain cultural sovereignty of the Länder with regard to any measures taken by federal organs and agencies, as well as to see to it that their politico-cultural work is in no way restricted.

In 1949 the West German Conference of Rectors (Westdeutsche Rektorkonferenz—WRK) was formed as an academic counterpart to the KMK. The WRK was composed of all institutions of higher education that are vested with the right to grant doctoral degrees and the *Habilitation*. Twenty-five universities and technical universities, as well as some theological seminaries, were represented on the original WRK. In the beginning of the 1970s all institutions of higher education at the tertiary level were allowed to join. In 1976, membership had risen to 156 institutions of higher education. The number of votes assigned to each institution differs according to the type of institution. Institutions that are authorized to grant doctoral degrees are guaranteed the majority vote in all committees. Table 3 lists the number of members and their voting strength:[4]

According to the 1976 Regulations of the WRK the member institutions are required to maintain constant collaboration in the areas of research, teaching, and studies, and tend to their mutual interests. Such goals very much resemble, in their general formulation, those of the KMK. Decisions of the WRK are reached by simple majority and merely represent suggestions to the member institutions. Specifically, the objectives of the WRK are the following:[5]

— to effect a common solution of the problems concerning the institutions of higher education;
— to present to the public the tasks, needs, and desires of the institutions of higher education, as well as the working conditions peculiar to them;
— to advise by recommendation the responsible political decision makers in the legislative and in the executive branches of government;
— to observe and to document developments in the area of higher education, and to report on such developments to the member institutions;
— to cultivate cooperation with state bodies, with other scientific organizations, and with associations and committees dealing with educational policy;
— to represent its members in international and supranational organizations and institutions;
— to assure cooperation with conferences of university heads or similar representative groups in other countries.

The recommendations on higher education policy made by the WRK are observed both by the public and the pertinent planning authorities as indicators of current conditions and trends in higher education. In many cases, the WRK has become active as an advisor on appropriate subjects. Examples of particularly important statements were the "Godesberg Statement of Rectors on Reforms of the System of Higher Education" of January

TABLE 3
The Members of the West German Conference of University Rectors, 1976

Type of Institution	Number	Voting Strength	
		Senate	Plenum
Universities, Teachers' Colleges, Comprehensive Institutions of Higher Education Authorized to Grant Doctoral Degrees	64	19	64
Teachers' Colleges not Authorized to Grant Doctoral Degrees	11	1	2
Fachhochschulen	56	3	11
Art Academies	16	1	2
Theological Seminaries	6	1	2
Other Institutions of Higher Education	3	1	1
Total	156	26	82

1968, and the "Alternative Theses to the Frame Law for Higher Education" of 1970.

When the first draft of the frame law was under discussion, the WRK suggested that a legally substantiated planning function should be given to a conference of institutions of higher education on the federal level. In its "Alternative Theses to the Frame Law for the System of Higher Education" the WRK gave, in May 1970, the following reasons among others for such participation in planning procedures: "In view of a developing shift of power from the parliaments to the executive, the West German Conference of Rectors considers alternative planning by a planning organization of institutions of higher education a necessary corrective vis-á-vis the executive."[6] However, in the subsequent process of elaborating the frame law no allowance was made for such participation. This incident brings into focus the problematic shifts of power among the areas of higher education, the executive, and the legislative—changes which are the necessary result of the gradual formation of a planning system that causes those institutions that are not involved to fear a lag in information and a loss of authority.

It should be mentioned in passing that shortly after the establishment of the WRK two other national institutions of academic self-government were founded which were based on old traditions: the German Academic Exchange Service in 1950, and the German Research Association (Deutsche Forschungsgemeinschaft—DFG) in 1951. In the German Academic Exchange the institutions of higher education are represented through their rectors and student bodies. The DAAD handles almost the entire academic exchange with foreign countries that is supported by public means. In 1976, approximately 7,900 foreign students and 940 scholars, as well as 3,300 German students and 800 scholars participated in the various programs.[7]

The German Research Association (DFG) is an association of universities, academies of science, and important scientific societies (e.g., the Max Planck Society). The DFG has become the decisive body for financing research in higher education. It considerably supplements the research funds of the institutions of higher education budgeted by the Länder. Since the DFG is an autonomous, central institution of research, it affords universities the opportunity to expand their research with additional money from funds administered centrally by representatives of the universities and research institutions, besides the basic financing they receive on a decentralized basis from the ministries of culture. In 1976, the budget of the DFG amounted to approximately DM 650 million; of this, 57 percent was funded by the federal government, and 42 percent by the Länder.[8] (The role of the DFG in supporting research in higher education will be discussed in more detail in Chapter 6.)

In the first decade after World War II, which we call the reconstruction phase of the system of higher education, both the institutions themselves and the system of higher education developed virtually without systemwide central planning. The primary function of the two central coordinating bodies—the Conference of the Ministers of Culture and the West German Conference of Rectors—was to serve as a forum for communicating the interests of their members.

Systemwide Initiatives, 1957–1969

Only after having attained the former status quo, when the individual institutions of higher education had once again become functional by reverting to old traditions, did the sector of higher education gain the interest of the public, even though initially attention was directed mainly toward research and its international competitiveness and not toward the already apparent excessive growth in enrollment.

According to the 1949 Königstein Agreement among the Länder, the financing of university research and systemwide research bodies (above all of the German Research Association and the Max Planck Society with its own institutes) were essentially the responsibility of the Länder. Since 1956, the federal government has taken part in the financing of these research bodies and the expansion of universities of higher education.

The large economic enterprises built their own research departments, often with the help of public funds. Various federal and Länder ministries initiated their own departmental research. When the technical, financial, and political aspects of atomic and space research became clearer, this inevitably led to the creation of a ministry on the federal level—the Federal Ministry for Atomic Issues—which was founded in 1955. It gradually became, in 1969, the Federal Ministry for Education and Science (Bundesministerium für Bildung und Wissenschaft—BMBW), and in 1972 the Federal Ministry for Research and Technology (Bundesministerium für Forschung und Technologie—BMFT) was created as a separate agency.

In view of the uncoordinated mushrooming of research facilities and, simultaneously, the favorable financial position of the Bund (reserve funds in the so-called "Julius Tower" were increasing) a long-term plan for science was called for.[9] Its establishment and continuous development was to be ensured by a central organization—the Science Council (Wissenschaftsrat), which was set up in 1957 through an administrative agreement between the Bund and the Länder. In addition to the Bund and the Länder (KMK) other lobbyists for the Science Council were politicians of all parties, and, above all, the German academics represented by their important autonomous organizations—the "Holy Alliance" of the German Research Association, the West German Conference of Rectors, and the Max Planck Society.

The Science Council represented the first central agency in which the Bund and the Länder worked together as such; at the same time, cooperation between the state and academics was institutionalized. The significance of the formation of the Science Council may be gauged from the fact that the scientific members are appointed by the President of the Republic, and he also issued the invitations for the first session. One reason for such a procedure may have been that the Länder wanted to avoid the preponderance of the federal bureaucracy and therefore preferred to have the President, as a higher office, issue the invitations, rather than a federal agency. This indicates how precarious it was to institutionalize cooperation between Bund and Länder.

The Science Council has thirty-nine members who work together in two commissions: the Administrative Commission and the Science Commission. The Administrative Commission is made up of the representatives of the eleven Länder (usually ministers of culture) and of six representatives of the Bund (with eleven votes). The Science Commission consists of sixteen scientists appointed by joint proposal of the West German Conference of Rectors, the German Research Association, and the Max Planck Society, as well as six persons from public life who are appointed by joint proposal of the Bund and the Länder. The division of labor between the two commissions is frequently characterized as follows: the Science Commission is responsible for that which is desirable, while the Administrative Commission is responsible for that which is possible. It must be said, however, that the administrative side also participates actively in determining policy. The Science Council has always been chaired by an academic. Any decisions of the individual commissions and of the General Assembly require a two-thirds majority vote.[10]

The Science Council only makes recommendations which theoretically are not binding for the Bund and the Länder. In reality, however, such recommendations have had a great impact because representatives of the advised ministries of the Bund and the Länder actively participate in the council's decisions. The functions of the Science Council are as follows:[11]

— To draw up an overall plan for the advancement of science on the basis of plans worked out by the federal and state governments within the limits of their jurisdiction; in so doing, the plans of the federal and state governments are to be reconciled, and main points and urgent needs must be defined.
— To draft an annual program of urgent operations;
— To make recommendations concerning the utilization of funds made available by the federal and Länder budgets for the advancement of science.

Despite its original terms of reference, the Science Council has, as of today, not worked out a general plan for the advancement of science; it probably was unable to do so because, as the first chairman emphasized, no plans to be combined in an overall plan have yet been submitted by the federal and state governments.[12] Rather, the main interest of the Science Council was soon directed toward the expansion and development of the system of higher education. In that activity, it could neither rely on particularly helpful statistical data or preliminary work in educational research, nor on appropriate concepts for planning. Hence the Science Council has done pioneer work in several respects. In the two decades of its existence the Science Council has worked out and decided on a wealth of recommendations concerning the general design and individual problems of the system of higher education.

The formation of the Science Council, and the federal subsidies for research and the expansion of higher education were only minor steps in the slow but steady increase of centralist tendencies which ran counter to the ideas of strict federalists. A controversy that took place at the beginning of the sixties concerning the constitutionality of a television station created by the Bund, and its treatment before the Federal Constitutional Court once again clearly outlined the two fronts. The Federal Constitutional Court itself censured the Bund for its unfriendly attitude toward the Länder and once again emphasized explicitly the cultural autonomy of the Länder. The Court gave the following reasons, among others, for its decision:[13]

> According to the basic decision of the Basic Law (Articles 30, 70ff. and 83ff., Basic Law) any cultural affairs that can be administered and controlled by the state are under the jurisdiction of the Länder, unless special regulations of the Basic Law specifically define limitations or exceptions in favor of the Bund. This basic decision of the Constitution—a decision that was made for the benefit of the federalist structure of the state in order to divide authority effectively—prevents us from assuming that cultural matters are within the jurisdiction of the Bund unless an unequivocal regulation to make exceptions exists in the Basic Law.

Three weeks after pronouncement of this verdict, the Conference of Ministers of Culture demanded "that the federal budget refrain from taking any new steps toward involvement in cultural policy and that its involvement be reduced at the same rate at which the Länder are given the necessary funds for such purposes."[14]

The request to reduce the involvement of the Bund remained unanswered; on the contrary, in the sixties there arose quantitative and qualitative problems for the system of education in general, and specifically for that of higher eudcation, that demanded increased involvement by the Bund. The quantitative changes that took place between 1960 and 1970 were characterized by increased student enrollment (approximately from 300,000 to 500,000), increase in expenditures for institutions of higher education, and advancement of research from approximately two billion marks to approximately eight billion marks annually.[15]

Federal expenditures in the area of cultural policy were by no means "reduced" during this period; rather, as far as the institutions of higher education and advancement of research are concerned, they were increased from 151 million marks in 1960 to 1.5 billion in 1970.[16] These funds were used by the Bund mainly for the expansion of universities, advancement of research, and to provide financial assistance to students. In 1964 this practice received a contractual foundation when the federal and state governments reached an administrative agreement, because by that time the Länder were no longer able to carry alone the growing financial demands of the ever expanding areas of science and higher education.

In 1964—the same year in which the Bund made decisive inroads into the field of higher education because of this administrative agreement that was somewhat outside the Basic Law— the Bundestag asked the federal government for a "report on the situation and the measures taken in the area of educational aid and educational planning." After three years' work—a process that was hampered by the inexperience of the federal administration in this area and by possible problems in coordinating the twelve partners—the federal Chancellor and the Conference of Ministers of Culture of the eleven Länder submitted the "Report on the State of Affairs in the Area of Educational Planning" in October 1967.[17] The 500-page volume contains a report by the

Bund in which an attempt is made "to give priority to the overall economic and social development and its significance for the educational system;" it also contains a section concerning the Länder with a preface on cooperation, as well as eleven separate reports by the Länder "because in spite of growing uniformity, the specific characteristics in the development of each individual Land were to be brought out."

The report of the Bund already contained most of the arguments for the amendment to the Basic Law introduced two years later which increased the authority of the Bund. It says in part: "Before any final decision as to what educational planning means can be reached, the federative structure of the Federal Republic requires close scrutiny. Special consideration should be given to the problem of how the participants, beyond present cooperation, can most efficiently contribute to planning in the area of education."[18]

The following remarks by Baden-Württemberg may stand for the summary statements of the Länder. They clearly draw the lines within which systemwide educational planning in the federative Federal Republic must operate:[19]

> Experience up till now in the area of educational planning has shown that "cultural federalism" is a valuable means to save planning from the danger of regimentation. It also shows, however, that merely "looking inward" is not sufficient. Educational planning of a Land needs to be supplemented by systemwide and international considerations if it is to meet the expectations of the modern world.

It is, however, questionable from the point of view of today's institutions of higher education whether central planning on the Land level is less endangered by regimentation than planning on the federal level.

Cooperative Federalism, Since 1969

The report on educational planning to the Bundestag clearly indicates the need for central governmental planning in addition to decentralized planning by the Länder. At the same time, this report to the Bundestag signals the growing involvement of the Bundestag in national educational policy and planning. With that, the period of a generally decentralized policy of higher education comes to an end.

In view of the advantages of cultural federalism and the strong preference of the Länder for it, the question arises whether the Länder could not have succeeded to cope with the task of central planning themselves without the involvement of the Bund. It is sometimes argued that this was not possible because of the procedural and indeed constitutional problems that impede central decision making by representatives whose legitimacy is based on decentralized authority. Also, the growing need for financial investments, in particular for the expansion of higher education facilities, would have required a redistribution of taxes in favor of the Länder in order to enable them to perform this task. Even if the Länder had come forth with convincing procedures for systemwide planning, it seems doubtful whether the federal Parliament would have agreed to a renunciation of income and thus of influence.

The trend to strengthen the federal authority was supported, to a significant degree, by the politico-social maxim laid down in the Constitution that uniform living conditions in all areas of the Federal Republic should be maintained.[20] (This point implies a centralist principle contradicting the perspective of cultural federalism which tries to preserve diversity).

In 1969, the Basic Law was amended by introduction of the common tasks (*Gemeinschaftsaufgaben*) between the Bund and the Länder. The common tasks were intended to involve the Bund in those responsibilities of the Länder which are important for the general public and in which the cooperation of the Bund was necessary in order to bring about uniform living conditions throughout the republic. Besides measures for regional economic policy, transportation policy, and agricultural policy, the common tasks concern education and science:

— Expansion and additional construction of institutions of higher education which were to be provided for by joint frame planning to be enacted in legislation (cf. Art. 91a of the Basic Law);

— The possibility to cooperate, by way of agreements, in educational planning and in the promotion of facilities and projects of scientific research of systemwide importance (cf. Art. 91b Basic Law).

Simultaneously, the Bund was authorized within the framework of competitive legislation to issue frame regulations on general principles of the system of higher education (cf. Art. 75, 1a Basic Law).

This amendment to the Basic Law represents a compromise which the federalists considered too extensive and the centralists too narrow. It was the work of the coalition government between CDU and SPD; in spite of its inadequacies, it offered the coalition between SPD and FDP that came into office in the fall of 1969 the chance for a new beginning in the area of educational policy, specifically of higher education, and was accompanied by great hopes and much skepticism. In 1969, in his policy declaration, the chancellor emphasized the outstanding significance which the Bund accorded to this newly acquired authority when he stated as part of his program "that knowledge and education, science and research are top priorities in the reforms we must effect."

The amendment to the Basic Law became the basis for federal participation in the tasks of educational planning; it also meant sharing a responsibility, particularly in the area of construction, which so far had been limited to cooperation in the recommendations for planning issued by the Science Council. Officially, the amendment to the Basic Law marks a turning-away from the principle of genuine cultural federalism. The term coined for this new form of cooperation between the Bund and the Länder was "cooperative cultural federalism."

In 1969, in order to tend to its new duties, the Federal Ministry of Scientific Research was changed into the more comprehensive Federal Ministry of Education and Science (Bundesministerium für Bildung und Wissenschaft—BMBW).* This

---

* From which the Federal Ministry of Research and Technology (BMFT) was separated in 1972. (*ed.*)

ministry represents the federal authority by acting as a "staff" or command post. In 1970 the BMBW submitted the "Educational Report 1970" containing the politico-educational program of the government. This program was characterized by reform enthusiasm and a favorable budgetary position. Both with respect to size and to quality, it surpassed most other programs, including those concerning higher education. Later, in the course of practical cooperation between Bund and Länder and the respective federal and state ministers, the scope of the program was cut down. With regard to the "Educational Report 1970," the Bund was told by its new partners that a program of this kind was, of course, welcome; however, the Länder objected to the fact that such a comprehensive and detailed program was submitted by the Bund alone and not in cooperation with the Länder; for in spite of the amendment to the Basic Law, the jurisdiction of the Länder over the system of education had been left largely unimpaired.[21]

The *common task of construction in higher education* was formally established in 1969 with the passage of the Higher Education Construction Act by which the Planning Committee for Construction in Higher Education (Planungsausschuss für den Hochschulbau—PLA) was created.[22] Members of the planning committee include the federal minister of education and science (chairman) and the federal minister of finance; there is also a minister from each Land, generally the minister of culture. Bund and Länder have eleven votes each. Decisions are made with a 75 percent majority. The planning committee makes decisions which are binding for the Bund and the Länder inasmuch as they must be incorporated in the annual budgetary draft. The final decisions are made by the parliaments, which must approve the budgetary draft and pass the budgetary law; this means that mutual frame planning by the executive of the federal government and the Länder may be ignored by their legislative assemblies.

For the *common task of educational planning and research promotion,* the Federal-State Commission for Educational Planning (Bund-Länder-Kommission für Bildungsplanung—BLK) was established in 1970 by an administrative agreement between

Bund and Länder.[23] The commission's functions not only involve the system of higher education, but also the entire area of education. The primary task of the commission is the development of a long-term plan for the entire system of education and plans for the necessary intermediary steps, as well as the establishment of a common educational budget. In 1971, its functions were extended to include coordination of pilot projects in the area of education through a frame agreement.[24]

The BLK consists of seven members from the federal government (with eleven votes) and one representative of each of the eleven Länder governments (eleven votes). Although the BLK is a governmental agency of the Bund and the Länder, it is, as opposed to the planning committee, not a decision-making, but rather an advisory agency that can only submit proposals. Hence, to outsiders the decision-making process for long-term educational planning appears rather cumbersome. The commission passes its recommendations with a 75 percent majority of the votes. Opposing members may record their dissenting views in minority votes. The recommendations of the BLK and the minority votes are submitted for decision to the heads of government of the Bund and the Länder. A decision requires the approval of at least nine heads of government. Only those who have agreed are bound by it, and only on condition that they have the agreement of their parliaments with respect to the budgetary consequences engendered by the decision. In the latter respect, the procedure is the same as that for the Planning Committee for Construction in Higher Education.

Since the frame agreement regarding common advancement of research[25] that was concluded between Bund and Länder in 1975, the commission has been called the Bund-Länder Commission for Educational Planning and Research Promotion. Whenever the commission attends to business that concerns the frame agreement for the promotion of research, a second representative of the Länder governments is present, usually the minister of finance. This does, however, not change the voting strength.

In compliance with the right granted to the Bund by the constitutional amendment to pass frame regulations for the system of higher education, the Frame Law for Higher Education (Hochschulrahmengesetz—HRG) was drafted under the direction of the BMBW. It grew out of the fourteen theses formulated by the federal minister of education and science in 1970[26] and went through several drafts until it reached its final form and was passed in the beginning of 1976. Even though the original version was greatly reduced in the course of parliamentary discussion, it was still the first time in the history of German higher education that a unified frame for the organization of the system of higher education was created. The laws of the Länder are to be adapted to it by 1979.

For the twelve years prior to 1969, planning in the area of higher education had been dominated solely by the Science Council, to a certain degree in the form of a dialogue with the representatives of the Länder and the institutions of higher education (KMK and WRK). With the planning functions of the BMBW and the two new commissions (BLK and planning committee) authorized by the 1969 amendments, systemwide planning was revitalized. Diagram B illustrates the development of the most important agencies for coordination and planning in the area of higher education.

DIAGRAM B
Significant Systemwide Planning and Coordinating Agencies in the
System of Higher Education, 1948–1977

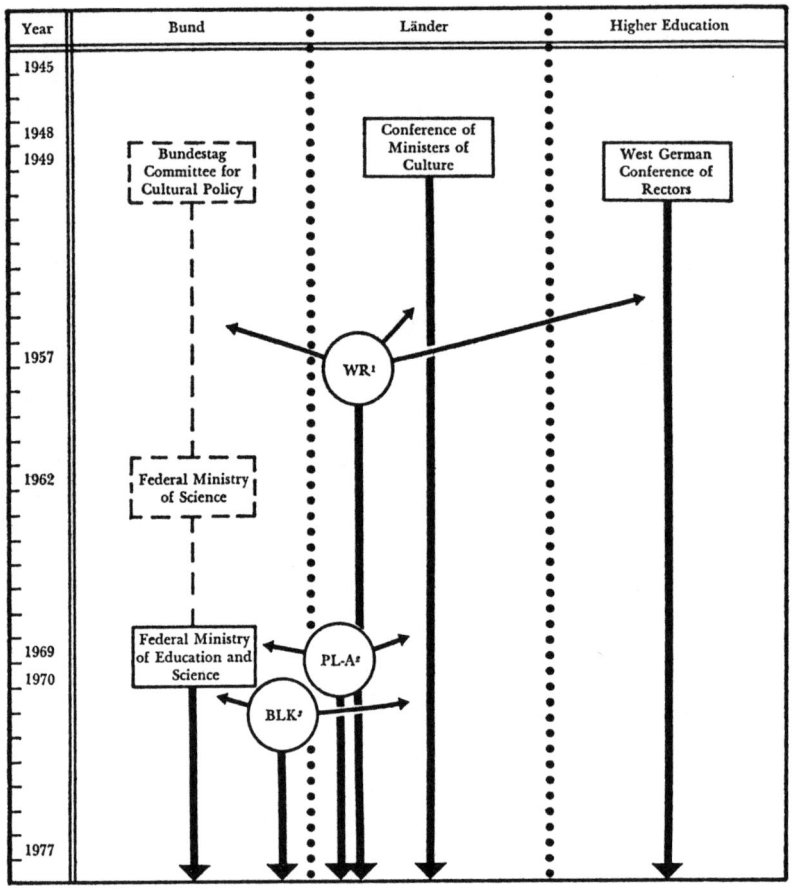

1. WR—Science Council (*Wissenschaftsrat*)
2. PLA—Planning Committee for Construction in Higher Education (*Planungsausschuss für den Hochschulbau*)
3. BLK—Federal-State Commission for Educational Planning and Research Promotion (*Bund-Länder Kommission für Bildungsplanung und Forschungsförderung*)

FOOTNOTES

1. In the three city states the heads of departments are called senators. In some Länder the responsibility for cultural affairs is shared by two departments, of which one is usually responsible for primary and secondary level education, the other for tertiary education.
2. For detailed information about the structure, history, rules of procedure, and focal points of the activities of the KMK, cf. Conference of Ministers of Culture, *Handbuch für die Kultusministerkonferenz 1974* (Bonn: 1974). (The handbook for 1977 is also in print); Conference of Ministers of Culture, *Kulturpolitik der Länder 1975 and 1976* (Bonn: 1977).
3. Conference of Ministers of Culture, *Handbuch 1974*, p. 75.
4. West German Conference of Rectors, *Arbeitsbericht 1976* (Bonn-Bad Godesberg: 1977), p. 11. For detailed information on structure, history, rules of procedure, and focal points of the activities of the WRK, cf. *ibid.*
5. *Ibid.*, p. 6.
6. West German Conference of Rectors, *Alternativ-Thesen der WRK zu den Thesen für ein Hochschulrahmengesetz des Bundes,* Documents for the reform of the system of higher education (Bonn-Bad Godesberg: 1970), pp. 60–61.
7. German Academic Exchange Service, *Jahresbericht 1976* (Bonn-Bad Godesberg: 1977), pp. 9–10. For detailed information about the structure, history, rules of procedure, and responsibilities of the DAAD, cf. German Academic Exchange Service, *Der Deutsche Akademische Austauschdienst 1925–1975* (DAAD Forum 7) (Bonn-Bad Godesberg: 1975).
8. For detailed information about structure, history, rules of procedure, and focal points of the activities of the DFG, cf. Thomas Nipperdey and Ludwig Schmugge, *50 Jahre Forschungsförderung in Deutschland. Ein Abriss der Geschichte der Deutschen Forschungsgemeinschaft, 1920– 1970* (Bonn-Bad Godesberg: 1970); German Research Association, *Aufbau und Aufgaben der Deutschen Forschungsgemeinschaft* (Bonn-Bad Godesberg); and German Research Association, *Tätigkeitsbericht 1976.* (Bonn-Bad Godesberg: 1977).
9. Gerhard Hess, "Ein langfristiger Plan für die Wissenschaft," *Frankfurter Allgemeine Zeitung* (July 5, 1956).
10. For detailed information about structure, history, the administrative agreement on the creation and the functions of the Science Council, cf. Science Council, *Wissenschaftsrat 1957–1967* (Bonn: 1968); and Rolf Berger, *Zur Stellung des Wissenschaftsrats bei der wissenschaftspolitischen*

Beratung von Bund und Ländern (Baden Baden: Nomos Verlagsgesellschaft, 1974).
11. Article 2 of the administrative agreement between Bund and Länder concerning the formation of a science council.
12. cf. Science Council, *Bericht des Vorsitzenden über die Arbeit des Wissenschaftsrates 1961 bis 1964* (Bonn: 1965), p. 8.
13. Federal Constitutional Court, Television Verdict of February 28, 1961.
14. Conference of Ministers of Culture, comments on the TV verdict of the Federal Constitutional Court; KMK press release on the occasion of the 81st plenary meeting on March 3, 1961.
15. Source for 1960: Willi Albert and Christoph Oehler, *Die Kulturausgaben der Länder, des Bundes und der Gemeinden 1950–1967* Hochschul-Informations-System GmbH, Hochschulforschung Volume 10 (Weinheim: Beltz, 1972), pp. 266–67—Expenditures for higher education, engineering schools and research institutes of the Bund and the Länder; and source for 1970: Federal Ministry of Education and Science, *Grund- und Strukturdaten* (Bonn: 1976), p. 122 (expenditures for institutions of higher education and general promotion of research in the educational budget).
16. Source for 1960: Willi Albert and Christoph Oehler, *op. cit.*, pp. 270–71; and source for 1970: Federal Ministry of Education and Science, *op. cit.*, p. 122.
17. German Bundestag, printed matter V/2166 (Bonn: October 13, 1967).
18. *Ibid.*, p. 6.
19. *Ibid.*, p. 315.
20. cf. Article 72, 3, and Article 106, 3 of the Basic Law.
21. Statement by the chairman of the cultural affairs committee of the Bundesrat, minister of culture professor Hahn, in the German Bundestag on October 14, 1970, during the debate on the Educational Report 1970.
22. For information on the common task regarding construction in higher education, the Higher Education Construction Act and the Planning Committee for Construction in Higher Education, cf. Peter Lichtenberg, Jürgen Burckhardt, and Dietrich Elchlepp, *Gemeinschaftsaufgabe Hochschulbau* (Comments and documentation referring to Higher Education Construction Act) (Bad Honnef: Verlag Karl Heinrich Bock, 1971).
23. For information on the responsibilities and the organization of the Bund-Länder Commission, its members and committees, as well as on the agreement, cf. *Information über die Bund-Länder-Kommission für Bildungsplanung und Forschungsförderung* (Bonn: 1976).
24. *Ibid.*
25. *Ibid.*
26. Reprinted in West German Conference of Rectors (cf. footnote 6).

3 PLANNING

One purpose of the amendment to the Basic Law of 1969 was the intent to lay the foundation for a coordinated development of the system of higher education. The resulting planning tasks are wide-ranging, from the "decreed" study reform to new admission policies, the determination of educational capacity, and focal points of research to the planning of construction, equipment, and personnel, as well as the financing of these matters. A meticulous system of planning procedures and mechanisms has been worked out in order to institutionalize comprehensive planning at all levels.[1]

Planning System

The basic elements for the system of planning were put into law in the Frame Law for Higher Education of 1976.[2] The Frame Law for Higher Education calls upon the institutions of higher education to set up "development plans" (Hochschulentwicklungspläne—HEP) which are to cover a time span of several years and be progressively extended. These development plans must specify the functions and the projected development of the specific institutions in the areas of research, instruction, services, and administration. They must also include plans listing the requirements of their organizational units. The requirement to furnish plans listing the needs of the lowest levels of administration brings in an entirely new aspect of managerial efficiency. These plans are to be structured in such a way as to allow a specification of costs arising in individual courses of study as well as an interinstitutional comparison in this regard. The Land is to establish general guidelines for this procedure. The development plans are the groundwork for the Land's comprehensive planning in the field of higher education and for the determination of the number of students to be admitted. After consultation with the institutions, the Länder are to work out a "comprehensive plan for higher education" (Hochschulgesamtplan—HGP) for several years hence which contains the present extent and the projected development both of the system of higher education of the Land as a whole and for each individual institution of higher education. The comprehensive plan must take into consideration intermediate-term financial planning, frame planning for construction in higher education, and the standards applied to determine educational capacities (according to Article 29 of HRG). Moreover, the specific requirements of regional planning must be taken into consideration. Taking into account the tasks of the Science Council and the Federal-State Commission for planning of higher education, the projected comprehensive system of planning is roughly illustrated by Diagram C.[3] The degree of realization of this ambitious planning system is more advanced on the higher than on the lower levels. So far, we can hardly speak of systematic long-term equipment planning at the departmental level; nor is it yet clear whether planning is to be done by the individual organizational units themselves, or by central university committees.

Also, the elaboration of institutional development plans by the universities themselves has not progressed very far. By 1975, only ten out of sixty universities and comprehensive institutions of higher education had worked out a development plan, but at that time almost all the institutions intended to begin working on those plans or were already in the process of doing so.[4] Teachers colleges, as well as *Fachhochschulen,* however, have only taken sporadic steps in the direction of development planning. One reason for this is the fact that up till now hardly any planning units existed in these institutions, while during the past years the large universities and comprehensive institutions have generally established such departments.

The institutional development plans that have been completed

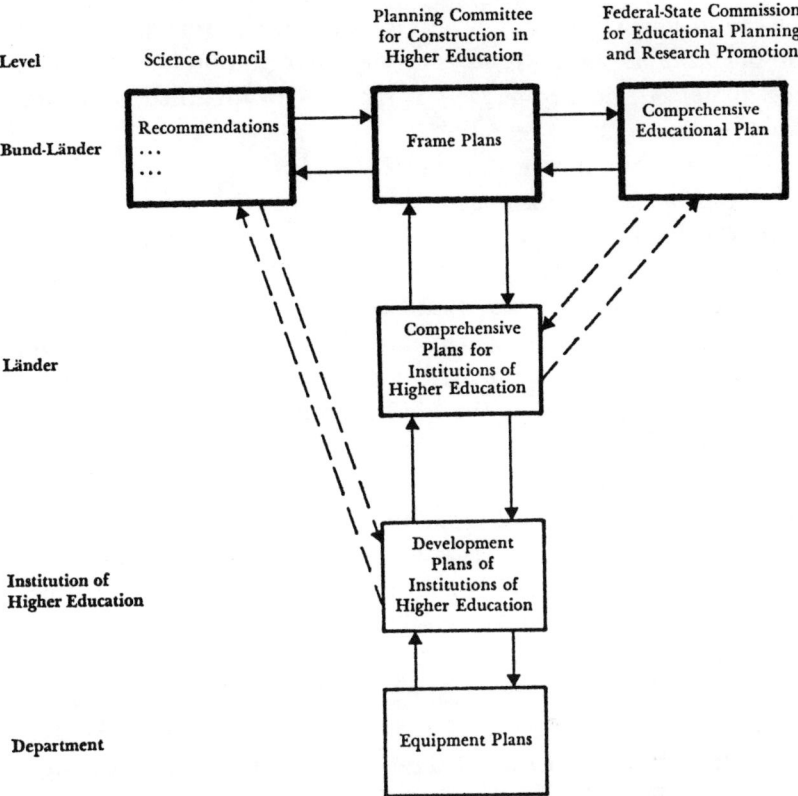

DIAGRAM C
The Developing System of Planning

or are in progress are pioneer efforts in the area of planning for higher education. They differ considerably both with regard to their priorities (objectives, structure, instruction, research, administration, personnel, teaching aids, space, and so on) and to their specific planning periods (between four and ten years). The plans for the development of the institutions of higher education represent, on the one hand, the instrument by which the institutions can express their ideas on their own development; on the other hand, the institutions are to specify and implement general planning objectives on the basis of previously issued guidelines. If necessary, they must identify discrepancies between their own and the general objectives of planning. In carrying out this procedure, the universities see the greatest problems to be the insufficient data they receive from the government—most of the Länder are still working on their comprehensive plans for higher education—as well as the lack of qualified personnel for this new field.[5]

In order to improve the shortcomings on these lower levels of planning, the Volkswagen Foundation initiated as early as 1969 the Information System for Institutions of Higher Education (Hochschul-Informationssystem GmbH—HIS), an agency that was taken over by the Bund and the Länder in 1976.[6] The HIS has contributed much toward the education of university planners. The focus of the HIS work is on the development of information systems and planning procedures for institutions of higher education. Since 1976 its activities have been mostly in the area of efficiency and the infrastructure of information systems, as well as studies of capacities and organization. The basic groundwork of the HIS has resulted in a great, sometimes confusing, number of models for university planning that at times present considerable difficulties to the planners who have to select and apply them locally. Yet it cannot be denied that the institutions of higher education that have evolved into large organizations are in need of streamlined control systems. Recently the BMBW provided a survey of control systems, their applications and requirements, for institutions of higher education, that covered no less than sixteen systems.[7] The complexity of these systems clearly indicates that institutions of higher education can no longer do without competent planning personnel.

On the Länder level systematic "internal planning" in the field of higher education began in the middle of the sixties. Baden-Württemberg was the pioneer. In 1964 it was the first state to set up a planning department in its Ministry of Culture, and already in 1966 it submitted its first model study for educational planning which anticipated supply and demand for the planning period until 1981.[8] The Baden-Württemberg Ministry of Culture listed its 1981 target to be a 15 percent quota of secondary school graduates qualified for university admission. At that time, this target seemed ambitious, but it has already been reached. Baden-Württemberg also was the first state to submit a comprehensive plan for higher education (1969).[9] Comparable attempts at comprehensive planning in higher education were the Great Hesse Plan and the North Rhine Westphalia Plan submitted in 1970. Other existing comprehensive plans are those for Berlin (1974), for Bavaria, and for Hamburg (both 1977).

In the meantime, all Länder are working on comprehensive plans for higher education, the preparations of which had already been required by most of the state laws for higher education and have now become obligatory through the frame law for higher education. More detailed guidelines for drawing up comprehensive plans are subject to state regulations. There are no uniform federal guidelines. Hence, legal guidelines as they exist for comprehensive plans for higher education in most Länder differ—in the same way as the development plans of the institutions themselves—in terms of content, planning period, procedures for progressive extensions, and methodology.[10] The mode of cooperation between the state and the institutions of higher education varies. It proceeds partly through informal cooperation, and partly through specific committees. Provision for decision making by the parliaments on the long-term development plan for higher education have so far only been introduced in three of the Länder (Bavaria, Berlin, Rhineland-Palatinate).

In order to create the administrative prerequisites necessary for planning in higher education, all ministries of culture have set up planning departments. In proceeding with their planning activities, these departments are subject to additional pressures resulting from the establishment of systemwide planning on the Bund-Länder level. Subordinate state institutions for planning and research assisting the planning department of the Ministry of Culture exist only in Baden-Württemberg and Bavaria. The creation of planning departments in the ministries of culture of the Länder is a clear indication that the primary authority for planning in higher education still rests with the Länder. This also becomes very clear, for example, if one considers that the systemwide Planning Committee for Construction in Higher Education can only deal with projects that are submitted by the

Länder. In principle, the Länder are free to plan and to build institutions of higher education without the agreement of the Bund or other Länder. If they do so, however, they will not receive any financial support. Theoretically, the Länder are exclusively responsible for personnel and equipment planning. There are, however, guidelines for long-term development in accordance with the comprehensive educational plan established jointly by the Bund and Länder.

Even though there is no question that the Länder still have primary authority for planning in higher education, the new central agencies that have been created at the level of Bund and Länder have the greatest impact on systemwide planning. We shall discuss, first of all, the work of the Federal-State Commission whose extensive tasks are an indication that frame planning for the system of higher education is not to be carried out in isolation, but rather in coordination with the entire system of education. Secondly, we shall discuss the planning committee that is responsible for construction planning in higher education institutions. Both commissions cooperate closely with the Science Council whose role as advisory agency for the system of higher education was, even perhaps, further enhanced by the creation of these new committees.

It also becomes apparent that the authority of the KMK as a coordinating instrument of the Länder has even gained in importance as a result of the planning activities on the Bund-Länder level. Moreover, the KMK acquired added responsibilities with regard to the increasing seriousness of problems connected with the *numerus clausus* and the reorganization of admission procedures (see Chapter 4). The same is true of the WRK. This agency, although it does not participate in systemwide planning, is challenged more and more by the results of central planning to express the views of the institutions of higher education. However, since KMK and WRK are not actually active in the planning of higher education, we shall limit ourselves to discussing the planning tasks of the Federal-State Commission and the Planning Committee for Construction in Higher Education, and to discuss those recommendations of the Science Council that affect systemwide decision making.

Plans of the Central Bodies

Comprehensive Educational Plan of the BLK

As we mentioned earlier, decision making in the Federal-State Commission (BLK) is a cumbersome procedure, and differences of opinion on party-political grounds between the members of the commission are considerable; yet in spite of these obstacles, the commission was able to accomplish the principle point on its agenda in an astonishingly brief time. Already in 1971 it presented its detailed interim report[11] which served as the basis for the Comprehensive Educational Plan (Bildungsgesamtplan) produced by 1973.[12] This plan covers the period from 1973 to 1985. In 1977, it was decided to extend the plan to 1990. The comprehensive education plan—just as the educational report of 1970—is based on the structural recommendations made by the Science Council and the German Education Council.* Although less broad in scope than the educational report of 1970, it contains an expansive, quantitative development program and general basic decisions about the structure of the educational system that is to be attained. Produced before the passing of the Frame Law for Higher Education, it was the first joint frame plan by Bund and Länder that stated the principles according to which structural and substantive reforms in higher education were to be accomplished.

The long-term educational policy upon which the Bund and Länder have agreed in the comprehensive educational plan can be read from the so-called structural quotas. For example, quotas were established for the proportion of new entrants in the population of the same age group, teacher-student ratios, the relation between students and study places, and the distribution of students in three and four-year programs.

---

* The German Education Council (Deutscher Bildungsrat) was set up in 1966 parallel to the Science Council as advisory body for the school system below the tertiary level. (*ed.*)

With the comprehensive educational plan, long-term planning of goals and cost calculation—which went far beyond the intermediate four-year financial planning practiced by the Bund and Länder—was introduced in the public sector. It shows clearly that an expansionary approach to educational policy can only be realized if the sector of education also has priority with respect to finances. It is obvious that such long-term planning is to a certain degree noncommittal. This is true of the objectives as well as of financial planning.

Long-term objectives may be changed by unforeseen developments and must have a certain measure of flexibility. With regard to the structural quota, for instance, it is not possible to anticipate with certainty how the ratio of new entrants will change. As to the envisaged division of courses of study into three or four years, the present development shows that it is not in line with demand and could only be attained through strict controls.

Financial planning depends on overall economic factors. It soon appeared that the comprehensive educational plan started out on too optimistic a prognosis so that certain reductions in financial demands necessary for reforms had to be made already when the plan was submitted. The noncommittal quality of long-term financial planning for an isolated public sector must also be seen against the background of financial and budgetary planning as it is practiced in the Federal Republic. Since 1967, the federal and state governments have had to present four-year intermediate-term financial plans which are revised annually. As such, they contrast with the annual budgetary estimates which are passed by Parliament as a budgetary law and hence are subject to legislative control. Intermediate-term financial planning, on the other hand, in which detailed plans of the individual sectors are coordinated, represents a declaration of intent by the government. Unlike the budget it is not legally binding since it is not passed by Parliament. Beyond intermediate-term financial planning, longer term systematic financial planning of public budgets either on the federal or state level does not exist in the Federal Republic. It is therefore not possible to make across-the-board promises to one ministry, particularly if other ministries have not yet handed in their plans for coordination.

The Federal-State Commission is dealing with the problems of necessary adjustments in objectives and financial planning by preparing the educational budget on the basis of a model that has a "what if" character.[13] On the basis of inputs of variable targets, this model permits calculations of personnel and space requirements, as well as of the costs of higher education and of the entire educational system. On the other hand, for a given input of maximum costs and personnel, attainable targets can be determined with this model. This was the way in which, for example, the first intermediate-term plan of the comprehensive educational plan was worked out by the end of 1974. The Intermediate-Term Gradational Plan for the Educational System until 1980,[14] which is essentially a cost and financing plan, required a complicated process of recalculation. The reasons for this were that the actual level the system of education had reached by 1973 was lower than expected and the overall economic development was also lagging behind projections; these factors restricted the expansion of the system of higher education as outlined in the comprehensive educational plan.

The comprehensive educational plan does not provide details on the state level; rather, as the Länder specifically emphasize,[15] it is a frame plan containing benchmarks for a uniform nationwide development of the system of higher education which allows the Länder creative freedom in educational matters in accordance with their authority:[16]

> One should not interpret the comprehensive educational plan as a law whose articles must be strictly adhered to . . . They are guidelines for educational policy, comparable to the guidelines in politics that are given out by the head of a government at the beginning of his office.

Frame Plans of the Planning Committee for Construction in Higher Education

While the comprehensive educational plan of the Federal-State

Commission contains the general long-term expansion targets for the institutions of higher education, the "common task" for construction in higher education calls for concrete cooperation between the Bund and Länder in the planning and realization of plans for the expansion of existing facilities and new construction of institutions of higher education, to which the Bund and Länder each contribute 50 percent of the necessary funds.

In order to carry out the common task, a four-year frame plan is worked out. This plan is revised annually and is to contain all the objectives and projects to be achieved unitedly in the area of higher education construction. The plan is characterized by a strict time table decreed by the Higher Education Construction Act. It requires the annual frame plan to be worked out after notification by the Länder by March 1 of each year. The Länder notifications are channeled through the BMBW which functions as the office for the planning committee to the Science Council. The latter must present its recommendations for the frame plan by April 15 of each year. The recommendations of the Science Council are the basis on which the frame plan is drafted by July 1 of each year. The first frame plan was issued in 1971, and it has been revised annually according to schedule.[17]

The object of frame planning is the provision and financing of "space-related" study places, that is, space that is required for each student in teaching and research ("Hauptnutzfläche pro Studienplatz"—HNF). Among others, this takes into consideration seminar and administrative space, seminar libraries, lecture halls, and laboratories, resulting from the requirements of the discipline and course of study, time budget, and plant utilization. The staff-student ratio and the resulting necessary space for personnel is also taken into account. The required space for special research areas and for central service institutions is determined separately.

The planning committee has worked out a detailed system of space and cost guidelines for frame planning which undergoes continuous refinement. The following table shows the standard values for the main utilized space per student on which the seventh frame plan for 1977 is based:

TABLE 4
Main Utilized Space Per Enrolled Student (Hauptnutzfläche—HNF)

Humanities	
University	4.0—4.5 qm
Comprehensive Institution	4.0—4.5 qm
Fachhochschule	4.0 qm
Natural and Engineering Sciences, Theoretical Medicine	
University	15.0—18.0 qm
Comprehensive Institution	15.0—18.0 qm
Fachhochschule	12.0 qm
Teachers College	5.4 qm
Art Academy	12.0 qm

With the help of these standard values for space per student, a simple division of the existing space can determine the available study places.[18] By multiplying the standard values with the number of study places to be available, the amount of construction still to be planned can be determined. The 1977 cost guidelines for the conversion of space planning into investment planning are shown in Table 5.[19]

The cost guidelines are later to be supplemented by guidelines for equipping buildings appropriately. The BMBW has commissioned a study of this question.

TABLE 5
Cost Guidelines 1977

Institutional Buildings	Building Costs DM/qm HNF	Overall Costs for Construction DM/qm HNF
Humanities	2.180.-	2.690.-
Physics, Electronics	2.640.-	3.280.-
Chemistry, Biology	3.730.-	4.630.-
Other Buildings		
Dining Halls	2.910.-	3.360.-
Residences for Nursing Personnel	1.790.-	2.300.-
Administrative Buildings	2.020.-	2.350.-
Sport Facilities (Gymnasiums)	1.620.-	1.880.-
Libraries (with more than 50% magazines)	1.650.-	1.900.-
Lecture Halls	3.580.-	4.420.-

The establishment and revision of the frame plan is closely coordinated with intermediate-term financial planning. The Higher Education Construction Act requires the frame plan to be worked out within the parameters of existing financial planning; on the other hand, as an element of intermediate-term program planning by the BMBW and the respective ministries of the Länder, the plan is part of financial planning.

It may seem to many outsiders that construction in higher education is a matter of technical routine. This may be the reason why the public has paid less attention to the frame plans of the Planning Committee than to the comprehensive educational plan of the Federal-State Commission. Such an attitude, however, ignores the true significance that the decisions of the planning committee have for the entire system of higher education. The significance of the committee's decisions may be gathered from the basic principles for higher education construction laid down in the Higher Education Construction Act. According to these principles, institutions of higher education, as part of the entire educational and research system, must meet future demands—a goal that is to be achieved by the common task. Bund and Länder are to see that:[20]

— the institutions of higher education form a cohesive system with respect to objectives, number, size, and location. This system is to guarantee a sufficient and balanced provision of educational and research facilities;
— research priorities be promoted in institutions of higher education in accordance with their respective objectives and by taking into account those research facilities that are not connected with institutions of higher education;
— construction meets the prerequisites for a balanced relation between research and teaching, as well as a functional structure of higher education and innovation in modes of learning;
— optimum utilization of existing and new facilities is guaranteed which takes into account projected student enrollment and expected long-term social needs;
— principles and goals of regional and state planning are taken into consideration.

With these principles, a quantitative building program is connected with far-reaching qualitative objectives. They require policy decisions that relate to the number of study places to be created, and to their distribution by region, by field of study, and by types of institutions. They even affect aspects of study organization if, for instance, decisions are made as to the ratio between large lecture halls and smaller seminar rooms in the buildings to be constructed.

In order to establish the parameters for construction planning, it is necessary to be guided by objectives which extend beyond the intermediate-term planning period. This is done in accordance with the longer term plan of the Federal-State Commission. However, because the frame plans for construction are revised annually and thus more regularly than those of the Federal-State Commission, modifications of objectives take place that affect the long-term comprehensive educational plan. An important example for this is the decision made in the sixth frame plan which departed from the projected goal in the comprehensive educational plan of achieving a balance between students and study places by 1985 and instead restricted building to 850,000 study places.

The Science Council's Recommendations

The Science Council was the first body to initiate overall planning of the system of higher education. It also was the assembly in which cooperation between Bund and Länder was tried out before such cooperation became institutionalized. It has been speculated that with the creation of the independent central agencies the Science Council would render itself, paradoxically, almost superfluous.[21] Experience has shown, however, that the Science Council has perhaps even gained in importance.

As we mentioned before, in the twenty years of its existence, the Science Council has directed its attention not so much to its original goal—a comprehensive plan for research—but has instead concentrated on recommendations for expanding and restructuring the system of higher education. Accordingly, its functions were reformulated in the extension agreement of 1975, which states the task of the Science Council to be as follows:[22]

> [The Science Council] is to set up, in study programs, recommendations for the development of institutions of higher education, science, and research, with regard both to substance and to structure. The recommendations must meet social, cultural, and economic demands. They should contain deliberations on their quantitative and financial effects, and on their implementation. Other tasks of the Science Council are those assigned to it by special decrees, specifically by the law for the advancement of construction in higher education. Furthermore, the Science Council has the responsibility of giving an expert opinion on problems of institutions of higher education, science, and research, if such opinion is requested by a Land, the Bund, the Federal-State Commission for Educational Planning, or the Permanent Conference of Ministers of Culture.

The Science Council's recommendations are of special significance for the common task of construction stipulated in the Higher Education Construction Act. According to these stipulations, the recommendations are to be the advisory gudielines for the formation and annual revisions of the frame plan for the construction of institutions of higher education. According to the procedure which has been established in the meantime, the recommendations contain basic considerations which are generally incorporated into the frame plans, and detailed evaluations of existing and projected space for each institution.

The objective of the planning committee is to reconcile its decisions with the proposals of the Bund and the Länder within the framework of a coordinated concept of planning. Through the activity of the Science Council, which systematically visits those institutions of higher education for which important building projects are at stake, the plans of individual institutions can be inserted directly into the deliberations of the planning committee—even if such proposals diverge from those of the Länder. This procedure constitutes an important balancing mechanism between the institutional and Bund-Länder levels which has been formally established in the developing system of comprehensive planning.

The structure and scope of the planning system may be summarized as follows: the comprehensive educational plan represents a design of long-term objectives for the system of higher education. However, to a certain extent, it is noncommittal since it is subject to unforeseen developments and to the latitude of the Länder's decision-making process. As to the development of university capacity, committal planning is done only by the Planning Committee for Construction in Higher Education with regard to physical expansion of institutions of higher education. The Bund-Länder agencies have no authority for planning personnel requirements which would be binding. Such planning is solely the responsibility of the Länder. However, it presents difficulties "because even intermediate-term obligatory planning of personnel in the public sector has never been done and is probably feasible only to a limited extent."[23] This is a decisive weakness of the systemwide planning procedure. If optimum utilization of available space capacity is to be ensured, space and personnel planning would have to be reconciled better. It is therefore intended that future building projects submitted by the Länder to the planning committee be accompanied by assurances that the number of personnel will be appropriate for the projected number of students. Such assurances, however, are not binding and are no substitute for intermediate-term personnel planning.

Data Gathering

One essential prerequisite for the efficiency of the evolving planning system and its planning procedures is the quality of statistical information and the educational as well as labor market data research that is to supplement it. These factors are the basis for forecasts about intermediate and long-term development. They represent important guideline data for planning decisions regarding the future system of higher education. In order to improve the notoriously deficient educational statistical data in the Federal Republic, at least for the area of higher education, the Bundestag passed the Law of Statistical Data for Higher Education in 1971.[24] Besides trying to achieve uniformity and to accelerate the process, the data-collecting program was to be extended in order to gain information on study patterns, length of studies, successful completion of studies, structure of personnel, as well as space and financial supplies in the institutions of higher education.

However, the implementation of this central program was fraught with so many problems that, in 1975, the West German Conference of Rectors found it necessary to make a public statement on "The Situation of Statistical Data in Higher Education." At this point, the federal statistical data on students had only been published up to the summer semester of 1972, while overall statistical data for personnel had been compiled up to 1973. The Federal Office for Statistical Data had not taken charge of gathering data on available university space until 1973; however, the groundwork had been done by the Science Council in 1971. The rectors made the following comments on this:[25]

> The reasons given by the statistical offices of the Länder and the Bund to explain the unsatisfactory state of statistical data for higher education are by no means convincing. It is unequaled in any other field of official statistical data in the Federal Republic. Personnel, financial, as well as technical and organizational problems are soluble just as in any other area of federal statistics. Hence, we cannot but have the impression that statistical data for higher education do not have the priority to which they are entitled in view of their significance.

Because of this situation, the WRK recommended to reduce the program in order to get at least some valid data. If this could not be done within a reasonable period of time, the WRK proposed to gather its own data from the member institutions as an emergency measure, "so that they would no longer have to rely on the statistical data of other agencies that were beyond their control.

The criticism of the WRK is very justified. It is only softened by the fact that in 1976, when the program had been reduced, the cross-section data of student statistics were for the first time published on time. With regard to data on the length and successful completion of periods of study, the planning agencies still have to rely on casual estimates of individual surveys. Until recently, such estimates were still based on such venerable "old-timers" of educational research as the examination of study patterns and study success of new entrants of the summer semester 1957.[26]

Because the statistical data is deficient, the work of the system-wide planning and coordinating agencies (BMBW, KMK, BLK, Planning Committee, Science Council, WRK, among others) is often based on diverging data sources and processing methods. Hence, their publications frequently contain confusing discrepancies in important data on higher education; obviously this complicates communication between the agencies.

In the past years, the BMBW particularly has issued numerous research commissions to overcome the statistical deficit and to complement the statistical data by adding qualitative information and case studies. These activities extend over a wide range of subjects, including forecasts of the demand of university graduates, investigations of educational attitudes, periodic questioning of students, university teachers, and the general population regarding key questions in the area of higher education.[27] However, it is evident that the infrastructure of the system of higher education itself is obviously not adequate for research of this kind. Frequently, commercial polling agencies were commission that are in a position to deal with the respective topics more quickly. Apart from these intermittent investigations, however, systematic continuous observation of the attitudes and behavior of school leavers and of students and staff in higher education, which is essential for planning in higher education, does not exist.

Pilot projects in the field of higher education, mutually supported by the Bund and Länder, also provide fundamental qualitative planning data for the reforms necessitated by developments in the system of higher education. In 1976, eighty-four pilot projects in higher education were carried out at a cost of approximately DM 35 million through the program of the Federal-State Commission (see Chapter 5).

The pilot projects range over a period of four to five years and the first results have just come in. The evaluations of pilot projects, and their translation into practical application at the institutions of higher education in the Länder are therefore only in their initial stages.[28] The BLK, however, has been rather hesitant to cooperate in this evaluation—a fact that leaves uncertain at this point how much the pilot projects may contribute to the planning of higher education in the Länder.

The sample data which the central planning agencies attempt to collect for their studies are partly supplemented by fundamental research conducted in a relatively small number of institutes for educational research in the Federal Republic. The investigations of the Institute for Regional Educational Planning in Hanover are an important basis for regional planning in higher education.[29] The Max Planck Institute for Educational Research in Berlin has carried out a number of individual studies in the field of higher education. One important focus of its research activities has been the connection between the educational and the employment system.[30] Among other topics, research on higher education is also conducted at the German Institute for Pedagogic Research in Frankfurt, Center I Educational Research of the University of Konstanz, the German Youth Institute in Munich, as well as some other research institutes within and outside of the universities. The institutes vary in their area of concentration. Some are engaged in more fundamental research, others in applied research, that is directly relevant to planning.

There is no doubt that educational research in the Federal Republic in general has gained in importance since the sixties. Yet even though the funds allocated to educational research have been considerably increased in the past years, they are still below average when compared with other countries.[31] The OECD analysts, for instance, considered the guideline which provided for a 2 percent share for educational research of the total costs for the educational system by 1985 to be utterly insufficient: "There is no major industry that could hope to keep up-to-date and competitive on such a meagre allocation, and in the case of education we are dealing with an activity that has a large deficit on the research and development account, accumulated from past decades of neglect."[32]

Planning Data

The most important benchmark data to be taken into account by the outlined planning system for higher education in the next ten years concern the development in the number of new entrants, students, study places, and academic staff.[33] Table 6, on the following pages, shows the development of these data in the last decade and a half.[34]

It is characteristic of the development until now that the extraordinary expansion of enrollment is not only the result of growing numbers of new entrants, but also of a considerable increase in the length of time the students remain at an institution. Even before 1970, this period was much longer than the suggested minimum length of study, and during 1970–75 it is estimated to have increased in university and university-type institutions of higher education by another 15 percent and in the *Fachhochschulen* by 10 percent (cf. Chapter 5 for a more detailed analysis of the problem of duration of studies).[35]

The increase in study places as related to space shows that through the united efforts of the Bund and Länder the expansion of institutions of higher education kept up with the increase in enrollment. The over-enrollment in the past years was kept within another 20 percent which the Science Council and the Planning Committee consider acceptable even for the coming years, after giving up the idea that by 1985 student numbers and study places should match.

Although the number of academic staff increased in the sixties, it has stagnated since 1974 and in 1977 personnel has even been reduced. All in all, therefore, the gap between students and staff widens, while study places have been increased at the same rate as enrollment. The following table shows how the staff-student ratio at the different types of institutions im-

TABLE 6
The Expansion of the System of Higher Education, 1960–1976*

Absolute data and index data (1971 = 100) Type of Institution	1960 Number	1960 Index	1971 Number	1971 Index	1976 Number	1976 Index
Universities (without educational sciences)						
Study Places	—	—	326,440	100	465,180	143
Staff Positions	15,552	31	50,227	100	58,305	116
New Entrants	46,600	62	74,900	100	95,715	128
Students	206,100	56	371,170	100	562,639	152
Comprehensive Institutions (without educational sciences)						
Study Places	—	—	1,900	—	28,595	—
Staff Positions	—	—	55	—	3,366	—
New Entrants	—	—			9,895	—
Students	—	—	2,570	—	42,852	—
Teachers Colleges (including educational sciences at universities and comprehensive institutions)						
Study Places	—	—	44,290	100	73,805	167
Staff Positions	1,112	22	5,138	100	5,180	101
New Entrants	13,400	46	29,200	100	10,945	37
Students	32,300	35	93,160	100	92,008	99

TABLE 6 (continued)

Art Academies					
Study Places	—	—	9,420	100	11,790	125
Staff Positions	435	34	1,279	100	1,604	125
New Entrants	2,600	76	3,400	100	2,573	76
Students	8,500	69	12,400	100	15,272	125
Fachhochschulen					
Study Places	—	—	86,300	100	108,930	123
Staff Positions	2,158	28	7,721	100	9,015	117
New Entrants	16,800	47	36,000	100	40,983	114
Students	44,200	41	108,080	100	142,679	132
Total					
Study Places	—	—	470,350	100	688,300	146
Staff Positions	19,257	30	64,420	100	77,470	120
New Entrants	79,400	55	143,500	100	160,109	112
Students	291,100	50	567,400	100	855,450	146

* This table is taken from the seventh frame plan for the construction of institutions of higher education which refers only to institutions included in the frame plan upon notification by the Länder. Total numbers are only slightly higher, e.g., for students in 1976 around 877,000.

proved from 1960 to 1970, while from 1970 on the relation grew somewhat worse because of the greater increase in student numbers. It should be mentioned that this is mainly due to a prolongation of the length of studies; the ratio between new entrants and academic staff has remained stable since 1970 with an average of 2.5:1.[36]

As far as future development in higher education is concerned, it must be assumed that, on the basis of demographic trends, the number of student applicants will rise considerably in the next few years and then decrease by the same rate over the following ten-year period. It is to be expected that 1984 will have the highest number of twenty-year old persons.[37]

Opinions differ, however, on the consequences this may have for the system of higher education. The most important "factors of uncertainty" in the estimates of student numbers lie in the variations of assumptions with regard to number of secondary school graduates qualified for entry to higher education and the actual enrollment quota, as well as the length of time a student remains in higher education.

TABLE 7
Staff-Student Ratio According to Types of Institution, 1960–1975

Type of Institution	1960	1965	1970	1975
Universities (without Medical Departments)	16.4	8.9	9.2	11.2
Comprehensive Institutions	—	—	—	12.9
Teachers Colleges	24.5	16.8	13.5	16.4
Art Academies	17.1	14.0	11.2	9.7
Fachhochschulen	20.5	16.8	15.4	15.8
Total	17.7	9.1	10.3	12.3

TABLE 8
Population of Twenty-Year Olds, 1970–1995

Year	Number	Index 1970 = 100
1970	825,700	100
1975	813,000	98
1980	947,000	115
1985	1,011,000	122
1990	774,000	94
1995	607,000	74

Ratio of Qualified Secondary School Leavers and Enrollment Quota

In 1976, the number of secondary school leavers qualified for entry to higher education comprised 22.9 percent of the eighteen to twenty-year old population.[38] Estimates of this ratio until 1985 vary between 23 and 27 percent:[39] the latest Conference of Ministers of Culture forecast assumes 29.4 percent for 1985.[40]

The proportion of the secondary school leavers qualified to enter as compared to those who actually entered institutions of higher education (enrollment quota) was 91.6 percent in 1975; in 1976, it decreased for the first time to only 83.1 percent.[41] Estimates of enrollment quotas until 1985 vary between 75 and 95 percent. According to estimates by the Science Council, the proportion of the number of new entrants to the eighteen-year old population will be between 17.8 and 26.3 percent in 1985.[42]

The enrollment quota is determined by many factors. The most important among them in the coming years are the *numerus clausus* situation, developments in the labor market, employment prospects in individual professions, and the opening of attractive alternative means of education outside the institutions of higher education. To some extent these factors have also an anticipatory effect on individual decisions with regard to which type of secondary education is sought.

Duration of Study

Besides the number of new entrants, the length of study at institutions of higher education is also an important factor for estimating the expected number of students. It is dependent on three factors.

Proportion of Students in Short-Term and Long-Term Programs of Study. Short-term programs (*Kurzstudiengänge*—K) last for three years. Long-term programs of study (*Langstudiengänge*—L) require four or more years of study. The present ratio of short to long-term students is 1:1.2.[43] Estimates for future development are based mainly on the assumption that demand for long-term programs of study will rise and that the ratio between short-term (*K*) and long-term (*L*) will reach 1:1.5, with *K* comprising 40 percent of enrollments and *L* totalling 60 percent.[44]

Student Drop-out Rate. In the past ten years the rate of drop-outs has been reduced from approximately 25 percent to approximately 12 percent of all entering students.[45] The BMBW's model calculations for the coming years assume a further reduction, according to which the rate of drop-out students in short-term programs would be 5 percent, and that in long-term programs 8 percent.[46]

Actual Average Annual Length of Study. In 1975, the average length of study was estimated to be 6.1 years for universities and university-type institutions (including three-year programs at teachers colleges) and 3.4 years for *Fachhochschulen*.[47] Estimates for the coming years vary between 3.8 years for short-term and 6.5 years for long-term studies (according to the present trend and a reduced proportion of drop-out students), and a period of 3.3 years for short-term and 4.8 years for long-term studies according to the regulations for time limits for the duration of studies stipulated in the Frame Law for Higher Education.[48]

This comparison of estimates of the present situation and assumptions for future development on the basis of forecasts by the various central planning agencies indicate the range of variations and hence the uncertainty of estimates for the development of student numbers in the next decade.

Diagram D illustrates the upper and the lower limits of the numbers of new entrants from 1975 to 1985 as described by the Science Council.[49]

Student numbers are shown in the forecast by the Conference of Ministers of Culture of 1977. They assume an increase of qualified secondary school leavers to 29.4 percent by 1985 and an enrollment quota of around 90 percent which varies from year to year. Their highest estimate for the duration of studies is based on the status quo. If one assumes that the regulations limiting the period of study imposed by the Frame Law for Higher Education are followed, then, according to the highest estimate for 1985, the number of students would decrease from 1,381,000 to 1,254,000. The diagram also indicates the upper and lower limits of the forecast by the Federal Ministry of Education and Science. In its upper limit, it corresponds with the KMK's estimate of the proportion of qualified secondary school leavers in the eighteen-year old population. In its lower limit it assumes a 5 percent lower proportion; that means that the 1976 enrollment quota of almost 23 percent would not rise much further. Furthermore, the BMBW bases its forecasts for both limits on the assumption that the decreased 1976 enrollment quota of 83 percent will remain constant, and that as of 1978 the duration of studies will conform to the regulations for time limits set forth in the Frame Law for Higher Education. In one respect, at least, all forecasts agree: after 1985 it is to be ex-

DIAGRAM D
Study Places, Academic Staff, Student Applicants, and Students, 1970–1985

Data for 1985:
- 1,381,400 (KMK)
- 1,254,300 (KMK)
- 1,021,000 (BMBW)
- 945,000 (BMBW)
- 850,000 (PL-A) — STUDY PLACES
- 271,410 (WR)
- 183,860 (WR) — APPLICANTS
- 121,600 (BGPL)
- 77,500 (status quo) — ACADEMIC STAFF

STUDENTS

actual development — prognoses

KMK = Conference of Ministers of Culture
BMBW = Federal Ministry of Education and Science
PLA = Planning Committee for Construction in Higher Education
WR = Science Council
BGPL = Comprehensive Educational Plan

pected that student numbers will decrease, after a certain time lag, following the decrease of new entrants due to demographic trends.

Diagram D shows the parameters within which quantitative development of student numbers is expected to take place in the years to come. Since educational policy is mostly oriented to individual demand, planning of space and personnel capacities must be based on these data. Because of the structure and the authority of the planning system, definite planning decisions have been made with regard to the expansion of existing facilities. As far as educational personnel is concerned, however, the comprehensive educational plan only gives target values, the realization of which is uncertain due to the role of the Länder.

Space and Personnel Capacities

Educational Facilities

As we mentioned earlier, the Planning Committee for construction in Higher Education decided in its sixth frame plan to abandon the objective of the comprehensive educational plan, according to which the number of students and available study places should match by 1985. In 1975 the Science Council summarized the arguments for this decision as follows:[50]

— The present target values exceed the present financial capacity of Bund and Länder.
— The target values do not sufficiently take into account the birth rate and its effect on the number of student applicants and students after 1985.
— According to the target values, the number of graduates from institutions of higher education would be out of proportion to the labor market.

Because of these considerations, it was decided to create facilities for 850,000 students. From 1985 on the capacity of educational space is to remain stable, that is, that the peak of student numbers between 1980 and 1990 is to be "tunneled." On the one hand, this is to be done to avoid excess capacity toward the turn of the century; on the other hand, it means that in the coming years facilities will be overcrowded. If the forecast that the peak of student numbers will reach approximately one million is correct, the rate of overcrowding will be the same as at present, that is, around 120 percent. However, should the peak be higher, it will exceed that percentage: in the highest estimate given by the Conference of Ministers of Culture, it would reach approximately 160 percent.

These conditions of considerable overcrowding have engendered demands for a more economic utilization of facilities in higher education. This economic utilization refers to organizational measures to make better use of the available space and also to use the facilities of the institutions in the five months between semesters when no classes or lectures are given. Already in 1972, in imitation of foreign regulations, the Federal-State Commission decided to introduce an academic year with semesters that were noticeably extended.[51] Such a change would, however, increase the teaching load of the faculty and reduce the chances of the students to earn the money that they might need. For these reasons, an implementation of the decision is not expected in the foreseeable future and is, in fact, no longer seriously discussed.

If all the projects submitted by the Länder for the seventh frame plan are carried out, they would cover 91 percent of the targets set for facilities by 1981, and after completion of all projects, 96 percent of the target value of facilities for at least 850,000 students. Thus facilities for only 33,000 students remain to be created that have not yet been submitted to the frame plan.[52] It appears, therefore, that the task of creating the required study facilities is about to be accomplished; this means that the direction of the remaining expansion projects of the frame plans relating to distribution by region and field of study have gained in importance.[53]

As to the structuring by field of study, criteria must remain flexible. According to the principles of the common task of construction in higher education, the availability of places is to depend on student as well as labor market demand. This means that target planning in this area is connected with the estimates and prognoses of student numbers and of the labor market, both of which are, as we know, subject to considerable uncertainty and fluctuation. In view of the sudden oversupply of teachers, for instance, it is now planned to halt the expansion of teachers colleges and to "redefine" the use of existing facilities at teachers colleges. Such "redefinitions" may become necessary in other fields, too, because of changing demands of new entrants. A specific problem of such "redefinitions" concerns the specialized qualifications of educational personnel, and we do not know yet in which way those concerned will oppose such measures.[54]

The basis for regional structuring of facilities is the intent to balance the available study places in every Land with the university-age population in that particular Land.[55] The degree of expansion achieved so far (1977) still shows quite a variation with regard to the specific target values for the individual Länder. It ranges from Rhineland Palatinate, where only 61 percent of the target value has been reached, to Hesse where 98 percent has been achieved.

Once all the projects submitted for the seventh frame plan are finished, some Länder will have surpassed their target values, while others will still be lagging behind (see Table 9).[56]

Since the objective is to achieve a regionally balanced expansion of institutions of higher education, the Science Council considers a modification of the target values of the specific Länder unjustified. Rather, the council has urged the Lower Saxony, Bavaria, and Rhineland Palatinate Länder to make greater efforts.[57] The planning committee has concurred with the suggestions of the Science Council, although in milder terms. It has asked the Länder:[58]

> to look into the possibility of accelerating the realization of their goals by submitting those projects that have priority and have a direct impact on the available study facilities for the next frame plan.

TABLE 9
Existing and Projected Study Facilities According to Länder, 1976–1985 (based on 1976 data)

Land	Degree of Realization 1976 (in %)	Planned Degree of Realization until 1981 (in %)	Facilities after Realization of All Projects (in %)	Expansion Target 1985 = 100%
Hesse	98	103	112	71,000
Baden-Württemberg	94	95	97	136,400
Hamburg	90	94	98	35,000
Saarland	88	90	92	14,500
Schleswig-Holstein	85	92	94	24,000
North Rhine Westphalia	85	96	101	228,000
Berlin	82	99	105	53,300
Lower Saxony	74	85	87	92,000
Bavaria	66	78	86	140,000
Bremen	64	70	75	15,000
Rhineland Palatinate	61	79	85	45,000
Total	81	91	96	854,000

One reason for some of the Länder's delayed expansion in higher education, 50 percent of which is funded by the Bund, is that they are afraid of the long-term expenditures for the use of personnel and material which must be carried by the state budget. Therefore, a plan to include at least the cost of material in the funding system of the common tasks is being considered.

Staff Capacity

As opposed to the planning of space expansion, nothing definite can be said with regard to future availability of academic staff. The projected staff-student ratio gives some indication of staff planning. According to the comprehensive educational plan, the following staff-student ratios were to be achieved by 1985.[59]

The comprehensive educational plan calculated the demand of academic staff in 1985 to be around 121,600, based on the given student-faculty ratio and assuming that student numbers will total one million.[60] However, if one considers the fact that economic conditions have caused the Länder to adopt restrictive personnel policies, the present number of personnel at the institutions (77,500) will probably stabilize in the coming years. At present, even a cutting down of academic staff can be observed:

TABLE 10
Projected 1985 Student-Staff Ratios

Area	Students-Academic Staff Ratio
Medicine	
Six-Year Program	3.0
Three-Year Program	10.0
Natural and Engineering Sciences	
Four-Year Program	8.0
Three-Year Program	10.0
Teachers' Program	10.0
Humanities	
Four-Year Program	15.0
Three-Year Program	16.0
Teachers' Program	15.0
Central Facilities	
(computer center, library, etc.)	80.0

from 78,800 (1975) to 77,500 (1976). And in Baden-Württemberg, for example, it is planned to reduce the academic staff at the nine universities of the Land by about 5 percent in 1977–78.

Hence, it is to be assumed that the enrollment peak in the eighties will also have to be "tunneled" with regard to the capacity of academic staff. In terms of this, measures for more efficient utilization of existing capacities have been discussed and even taken (see Chapter 4), as well as additional measures for a temporary increase of teaching capacity. One such measure is the introduction of a temporary and voluntary "emergency overload quota" as proposed by the West German Conference of Rectors.[61] In view of the imminent emergency situation, the Hochschulverband, an association representing the professors in higher education, has reacted positively to this proposal. This indicates that many professors are prepared to cope with this emergency measure.[62]

The "efficiency report" of the Federal-State Commission on the "size and utilization of personnel capacity and teaching obligations in the area of higher education" presents a detailed analysis of the supporting, partly cost-related, measures to be taken in order to implement the temporary overload quotas in some disciplines. The measures include compensation for overtime and the temporary allocation of available funds to the departments for extra teaching appointments and for the employment of auxiliary personnel.[63] It should be mentioned that such measures can only be successful if the present distrust between government and higher education diminishes (see Chapter 7).

FOOTNOTES

1. On this point cf. for basic discussion Jens Hoffer, *Zur Problematik der Planung im Hochschulbereich.* Aspects of methods and organization in planning of higher education in the Federal Republic of Germany (Cologne: Carl Heymanns Verlag, 1974).
2. Cf. Frame Law for Higher Education, "Planning of Higher Education," paragraphs 67–69.
3. Adapted from Heinz Bolsenkötter (Wibera Project Group), *Ökonomie der Hochschule.* (A managerial analysis) (Baden-Baden: Nomos Verlagsgesellschaft, 1976), p. 56.
4. According to a poll taken by the HIS GmbH. Cf. Jürgen Fischer, Christoph Oehler and Jochen Pohle, *Hochschulentwicklungsplanung.* Concepts–Methods–Aids (HIS Letter 57) (Munich: Verlag Dokumentation, 1975), pp. 36 ff. Cf. also the detailed analyses in this book on the tasks and the situation of development planning of institutions of higher education.
5. Cf. *ibid.,* pp. 37–38.
6. For information on the HIS GmbH. cf. Hochschul-Informations-System GmbH, *HIS 1974–75 Jahresbericht* (Hannover: 1975). The work of the HIS GmbH has so far been published in three series: Series Research into Higher Education, Volumes 1–10 (completed); Series Planning in Higher Education, Volumes 1–27; Series HIS Letters, Volumes 1–60. These publications can be obtained through Verlag Dokumentation, Munich.
7. Federal Ministry for Education and Science, *Betriebsoptimierungssysteme für Hochschulen* (Series *Hochschule* Volume 21) (Bonn: 1977).
8. Hans Peter Widmaier *et al., Bildung und Wirtschaftswachstum.* Model study for educational planning (Villingen: Neckar Verlag, 1966). This work was published as the third volume in the series of the Ministry of Culture of Baden-Württemberg entitled "Bildung in neuer Sicht." The series was begun in 1965 and was an important factor when systematic educational planning in Baden-Württemberg and in the Federal Republic was introduced.
9. *Hochschulgesamtplan I der Landesregierung Baden-Württemberg,* Bildung in neuer Sicht, Series A, No. 18 (Villingen: Neckar Verlag, 1969). This was preceded by the report of the working group for comprehensive planning in higher education of the Baden-Württemberg Ministry of Culture ("Dahrendorf Report"), published in 1967 as *Hochschulgesamptplan Baden-Württemberg,* Bildung in neuer Sicht, Series A, No. 5 (Villingen: Neckar Verlag, 1967). Further development of the comprehensive plan for higher education resulted in 1972 in the *Hoch-*

schulgesamtplan II für Baden-Württemberg, Bildung in neuer Sicht, Series A, No. 27 (Villingen: Neckar Verlag, 1972).
10. Cf. the summaries by Jürgen Fischer, Christoph Oehler, and Jochen Pohle, *op. cit.* (Footnote 4), pp. 26 ff.
11. Interim report of the Federal-State Commission for Educational Planning to the heads of the federal and state governments concerning the comprehensive educational plan and an educational budget, Volumes I and II (Bonn: October 18, 1971).
12. Federal-State Commission for Educational Planning, *Bildungsgesamtplan,* Volumes I and II (Stuttgart: Klett, 1973).
13. The so-called "standard cost model" developed by the BMBW is based on twenty-six input data, the most important of which are the annual numbers of primary, secondary, and tertiary students. For a more detailed description of the model, cf. Federal-State Commission for Educational Planning, *Bildungsgesamtplan,* Volume II, *ibid.,* pp. 216 ff.
14. Federal-State Commission for Educational Planning, *Mittelfristiger Stufenplan für das Bildungswesen bis zum Jahr 1978,* Volumes I and II (Stuttgart: Klett, 1975).
15. Cf. e.g., Federal-State Commission for Educational Planning, *Bildungsgesamtplan,* Volume I, *op cit.,* p. 8; also *Mittelfristiger Stufenplan, ibid.,* p. 2.
16. Ernst Höhne, "Die Bund-Länder-Kommission für Bildungsplanung— ihre Gestalt und ihre Wirksamkeit," *Zeitschrift für Pädagogik,* Volume XX/Number 3 (1974), p. 363. For other works and current projects of the Federal-State Commission cf. Federal-State Commission for Educational Planning and Research Promotion, *Jahresbericht 1976* (Bonn: 1976).
17. Cf. Planning Committee for Construction in Higher Education, *Erster Rahmenplan für den Hochschulbau 1972–1975* (Bonn: 1971). The seventh frame plan for 1978–1981 was presented in July of 1977. The frame plans are among the most important documents for basic deliberations and planning procedures in the system of higher education.
18. So far, the Planning Committee has not yet issued any guide values for the required space for medicine, dentistry, veterinary medicine and agricultural sciences. For the time being, the determination of existing facilities is based on the present number of students.
19. Total construction costs are composed of building costs, costs for the development of the building sites, and costs for furnishings and equipment.
20. Higher Education Construction Act (Hochschulbauförderungsgesetz— HBFG), paragraph 2.
21. Cf Rolf Berger, *Zur Stellung des Wissenschaftsrats bei der wissenschaftspolitischen Beratung von Bund und Ländern* (Baden-Baden: Nomos Verlagsgesellschaft), 1974, S. 128.
22. Article 2.1 of the agreement between Bund and Länder to establish

a science council in the version of the extended agreement of May 27, 1975. Reprinted in Science Council, *Empfehlungen und Stellungnahmen 1975* (Cologne: 1976), p. 304.

23. Planning Committee for Construction in Higher Education, *Sechster Rahmenplan für den Hochschulbau 1977–1980* (Bonn: 1976), p. 13.
24. *Gesetz über eine Bundesstatistik für das Hochschulwesen* of August 31, 1971 (Law of Statistical Data for Higher Education) *Bundesgesetzblatt* No. 91 (1971), p. 1473 ff. Cf. also U. Meindl, "Amtliche Statistik als Datenquelle für die Hochschulentwicklungsplanung" in Jürgen Fischer, Christoph Oehler, and Jürgen Pohle (Footnote 4), pp. 214 ff.
25. "Zur Lage der Hochschulstatistik." Comments by the 116th plenum of the West German Conference of Rectors. November 10/11, 1975. West German Conference of Rectors, *Arbeitsbericht 1975* (Bonn-Bad Godesberg, 1976), p. 148.
26. Gerhard Kath, Christoph Oehler, and Roland Reichwein, *Studienweg und Studienerfolg*. Max Planck Institute for Educational Research, Studies and Reports No. 6 (Berlin: 1966).
27. Cf. Federal Ministry for Education and Science, *Leistungsplan Bildungsforschung und Wissenschaftsförderung* (Bonn: 1976)'.
28. Cf. Federal Ministry for Education and Science, *Jahresbericht 1976* (Bonn: 1976), pp. 36–37.
29. For objectives, tasks, and organization cf. Institut für Regionale Bildungsplanung—Arbeitsgruppe Standortforschung GmbH, *Jahresbericht 1975/76* (Hannover, 1976).
30. For information on current work cf. Max Planck Institute for Educational Research, *Tätigkeitsbericht 1975/76* (Berlin).
31. Cf. on this point Friedrich Edding and Klaus Hüfner, "Probleme der Organization und Finanzierung der Bildungsforschung in der Bundesrepublik Deutschland." Deutscher Bildungsrat, *Bildungsforschung*, Part 2. Comments and Studies of the Commission for Education, Volume 51 (Stuttgart: Klett, 1975).
32. OECD, Review of National Policies for Education (Paris, 1972), pp. 91–92.
33. We already mentioned that, as far as the informational basis is concerned, the central agencies frequently work with varying data sources and processing methods which frequently result in confusing discrepancies. When compiling frame data for the past and future development in this chapter, we had to use different sources, and we often found discrepancies that could not always be explained. In each case, we chose the source that seemed appropriate for the context.
34. Cf. Planning Committee for Construction in Higher Education, *Siebter Rahmenplan für den Hochschulbau 1978–1981* (Bonn: 1977), p. 10.
35. Cf. Federal-State Commission for Educational Planning and the Advancement of Research, *Untersuchungen über die Effizienz im Bildungswesen*. Appendix No. 2: "Verweildauer im Hochschulbereich" (Bonn: 1976), p. 3 (in the following quoted as *Effizienzbericht*).

36. Cf. Science Council, *Empfehlungen zum Siebten Rahmenplan für den Hochschulbau 1978–1981*. (Koln: 1977), p. 49.
37. Population estimate 1975–1995 by the Federal Office for Statistics, quoted from Science Council, *Empfehlungen zu Umfang und Struktur des Tertiären Bereichs* (Cologne: 1976), pp. 22 ff.
38. Cf. Communications and Information by the Secretariat of the Conference of Ministers of Culture No. 4/77, July 15, 1977.
39. Cf. Science Council, *op. cit.* (footnote 37), pp. 23 ff.
40. Prognosis of the data commission of the Conference of Ministers of Culture of January 24, 1977, (in the following quoted as KMK-Prognosis), p. XV.
41. According to an unpublished document of the Federal Ministry for Education and Science about the development in numbers of new entrants and students, April 1977 (in the following quoted as BMBW Document).
42. Assumptions for the proportion of 17.8 percent new entrants: quota of qualified secondary school graduates = 23 percent, enrollment quota = 75 percent; for the proportion of 26.3 percent new entrants: quota of qualified secondary school graduates = 27 percent, enrollment quota = 95 percent. Cf. Science Council, *op. cit.* (footnote 37), p. 29.
43. Cf. *Sechster Rahmenplan für den Hochschulbau, op. cit.*, p. 9.
44. Cf. *ibid.*
45. According to a poll taken by the Hochschul-Informations-System GmbH.; cf. Federal Ministry of Education and Science, *Informationen* 5/77, p. 82.
46. Cf. Sechster Rahmenplan, *op. cit.*, p. 9.
47. *Effizienbericht, op. cit.* Appendix 2, p. 3.
48. Cf. Sechster Rahmenplan, *op. cit.*, p. 9.
49. Explanations and sources for Diagram D.
   — For actual development of student numbers from 1970–1976 and the two KMK forecasts for 1977–1978 presented cf. KMK prognosis of January 24, 1977, pp. XVII and XVIII. The two lower estimates correspond with the assumptions the BMBW considers probable (according to an unpublished BMBW document).
   — Available study places for students from 1971 to 1976 and planned targets for 1981 and 1985, based on the *Siebter Rahmenplan, op. cit.*, pp. 10 and 31.
   — Data on past student applicants and their alternative estimate until 1995 correspond to the assumption by the Science Council, *op. cit.* (footnote 37), pp. 110 and 111. The KMK prognosis of January 1977, also used by the BMBW, estimates that in 1985 the proportion of those qualified for entry will be somewhat higher (29.4%, rather than 27%) than the maxi-

mum estimate of the Science Council. The estimated enrollment quota is, however, below the maximum estimate of the Science Council of 95% (KMK at least 5% lower, BMBW 12% lower), so that neither the KMK prognosis nor the expectations of the BMBW go beyond the upper limit of the band.
— Data for academic staff from 1970 to 1975 from BMBW, *Grund und Strukturdaten* (Bonn: 1976), p. 102. For 1976 from *Siebter Rahmenplan, op. cit.*, p. 10. The higher estimate for 1985 corresponds with the target value of the comprehensive educational plan of 1973, *Bildungsgesamtplan, op. cit.* (Footnote 12), Volume 11, p. 39. The lower estimate corresponds to a stagnation of educational personnel on the level of 1977.

50. Science Council, *op. cit.* (Footnote 22), p. 189.
51. Cf. Federal-State Commission for Educational Planning, *Vorschläge für die Durchführung vordringlicher Massnahmen* (Stuttgart: Klett, 1972), p. 49.
52. Cf. *Siebter Rahmenplan, op. cit.*, p. 29.
53. Cf. especially Science Council, "Regionale und fachliche Strukturierung des weiteren Ausbauprogramms für die Hochschulen," *op. cit.* (Footnote 22), pp. 187–256.
54. Cf. *Siebter Rahmenplan, op. cit.*, p. 18.
55. Cf. Science Council, *op. cit.* (Footnote 22), pp. 198–99. For the concept of regionalization cf. also K. J. Luther and D. Swatek, "Regionalisierung der Gemeinschaftsaufgabe Hochschulbau" in *Informationen zur Raumentwicklung*, No. 3/4, 1977.
56. Cf. *Siebter Rahmenplan, op. cit.*, p. 31.
57. Cf. Science Council, Empfehlungen zum siebten Rahmenplan für den Hochschulbau *op. cit.* (Footnote 36), pp. 85–86.
58. *Siebter Rahmenplan, op. cit.*, p. 30.
59. Cf. *Bildungsgesamtplan, op. cit.*, Volume I, p. 47.
60. Cf. *Bildungsgesamtplan, op. cit.*, Volume II, p. 39.
61. Cf. West German Conference of Rectors, *Arbeitsbericht 1976* (Bonn-Bad Godesberg, 1977), Appendix 24 "Zur begrenzten Überlastung der Hochschulen in den Jahren der verstärkten Nachfrage nach Studienplätzen," pp. 175 ff., and Appendix 27 "Zur Einführung eines Notzuschlags auf Zeit (Zusatzlast) zur Erweiterung der Kapazitäten der Hochschulen während der Jahre verstärkter Nachfrage nach Studienplätzen," pp. 191–92.
62. Cf West German Conference of Rectors, *Qualität und Quantität—Die Hochschulen im Schatten des Studentenberges.* (Annual Meeting 1976). Dokumente zur Hochschulreform XXX/1977 (Bonn-Bad Godesberg: 1977), p. 38.
63. Cf. *Effizienbericht*, Appendix 1, pp. 21–22.

4 ADMINISTRATION

Finance

In 1970, the educational policy of the new federal government envisaged a greater increase in expenditures on education and science, compared with that in other public sectors, in order to achieve the newly formulated objectives of educational reform by the early eighties.[1] Since the Länder carry most of the financial burden for education—until 1969 the Bund funded only 6.3 percent of all educational expenditures—they could not be expected to meet the exorbitant rise in costs. Hence, to improve the general financial position of the Länder, the portion of sales taxes received by the Länder was raised from 30 to 35 percent, and provision was made to give additional federal funds to the financially weak Länder.

Another important condition for intensified expansion of the higher education sector was the participation of the Bund in investment for construction in higher education and research promotion. With the introduction of "common tasks" into the Basic Law in 1969, this participation of the Bund in financing higher education—which has already been practiced for some time—was finally legitimized in the Constitution.

This vertical equalization of financial burdens complies with the Federal Republic's subsidizing principle which requires that the higher political unit must share in those responsibilities that the lower political units cannot satisfactorily carry. Apart from this, there is a horizontal financial equalization between the Länder which requires the financially strong Länder to make equalization payments to those Länder that are financially weak.

With regard to the extent of equalization payments, the capacity of the system of higher education in the individual Länder has been brought into discussion. Those Länder that have a high "student import"—a high rate of students from other Länder—ask to be given credit for this "educational assistance" when financial equalization is determined. So far, however, their demands have not been met.

In 1975, as a result of these measures to equalize financial burdens, tax receipts and expenditures for higher education per capita in the eight Länder (not included are the city states Hamburg, Bremen, and Berlin) were as shown in Table 11.[2] This cross-section for 1975 illustrates the high and rather varying proportion of expenditures on higher education in the budgets of the Länder. Yet a very high proportion does not necessarily indicate a better equipped system of higher education; it may also indicate that during this period unusual efforts were made to reduce the lag in higher education, in order to unify standards of living as stipulated by the Constitution.

The proportional changes in the annual educational budgets and in the expenditures on higher education as compared to general public expenditure by Bund, Länder, and municipalities show the extent to which the federal government's 1970 intent to achieve a more than proportional increase in educational

TABLE 11
Tax Receipts of the Länder (Excluding City States) and Expenditures on Higher Education, 1975

Land	Tax Receipts DM per capita	Expenditures on Higher Education	
		DM per capita	% of Tax Receipts
Baden-Württemberg	1.346.–	212.–	15.8
Bavaria	1.293.–	165.–	12.8
Hesse	1.325.–	226.–	17.1
Lower Saxony	1.333.–	158.–	11.9
North Rhine Westphalia	1.334.–	184.–	13.8
Rhineland Palatinate	1.312.–	129.–	9.8
Saarland	1.371.–	235.–	17.4
Schleswig-Holstein	1.318.–	125.–	10.2
Total	1.326.–	181.–	13.7

expenditures was realized. Diagram E illustrates the rates of increase to 1975, using 1961 as the base year.[3]

Diagram E shows that the entire educational budget, as well as the expenditure on institutions of higher education, did indeed increase above average up to 1974. It should also be mentioned that the special concentration on educational policy as defined in 1970, especially for the higher education sector only accelerated the rate of above-average growth that had already begun in the sixties. This trend would have to be maintained if the Federal Republic wanted to approach the target of a 26 percent share of expenditure on education, science, and research in the entire public expenditure of 1985—a target recommended by the OECD analysts.[4] In 1975, the educational budget only comprised approximately 16 percent of the total public expenditure.

The same is true of the proportion of the gross national product. Here, too, the educational budget grew at a higher than proportional rate, from 2.7 percent to 5.4 percent, while expenditure on higher education grew from 0.5 percent to 1.3 percent. Incidentally, the OECD analysts considered the federal government's objective to achieve an 8 percent proportion of the GNP for the educational budget by 1980 to be normal and "not out of line with long-term trends in other modern countries."[5]

However, the above-average growth rate of the educational budget leveled off in 1974. This indicates to what degree the ambitious educational plan was dependent on economic conditions. Even though the proportion of the educational budget in the GNP still rose by 0.1 percent between 1974 to 1975, it decreased vis-á-vis public expenditure from 16.7 percent to 15.6 percent, while expenditure on higher education decreased from 4.1 percent to 3.7 percent. This coincides with directing increased attention to the development of vocational training on the secondary level which had been a rather neglected sector of education. In 1975, there were 840,000 students registered for the winter semester 1975/76 and 78,800 academic staff, and expenditures on higher education in 1975 were DM 13.5 billion. Of this sum, 58 percent was spent on staff, 19 percent on equipment, and 20 percent on investments.[6]

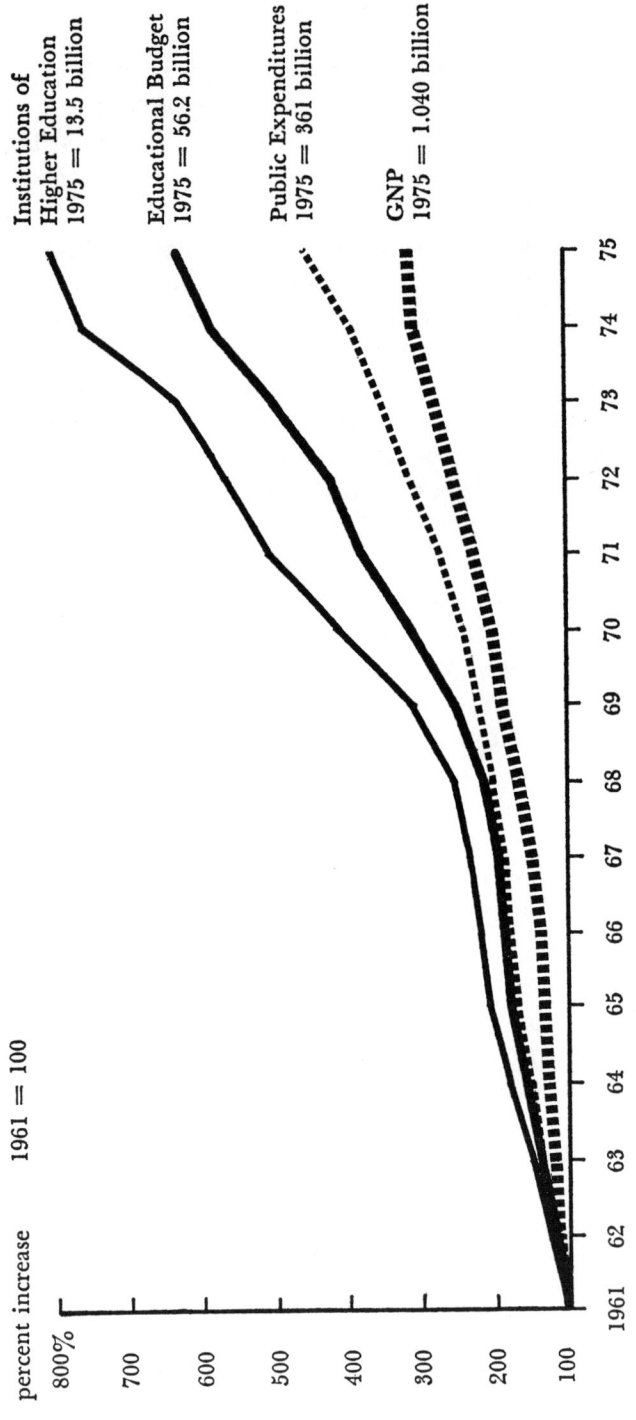

Table 12 shows the per student costs for 1975.[7] The costs vary with the types of institution and area of study; since comprehensive institutions are still in the developmental stage, their numbers must be examined with some reservation.

The longer students remain in higher education, the lower the average expenditure per student because of the higher number of students. If periods of study would conform to set standard times, the average expenditure per student would be higher.

Based on the present average of periods of study within one field (excluding the time spent in other fields as a result of transferring), the average cost per student for a complete study course at a university in the mid–1970s was DM 64,000 (ranging from law and social sciences with DM 14,400 to medicine with DM 240,000). At comprehensive institutions and art academies it was DM 45,000 and at *Fachhochschulen* it was DM 21,000 (according to the BMBW).

The financing of institutions of higher education, which except for a few are state institutions of the Länder, is assured by

TABLE 12
Expenditure per Student, According to Type of Institutions and Area of Study, 1975
(in DM)

Area of Study (and respective proportion of students in all institutions of higher education)	University, Teachers College	Comprehensive Institution	Fachhochschulen	Average for all Institutions
Humanities, Theology (27.4%)	4,900	3,300	4,700	4,800
Law, Social Sciences (23.2%)	2,900	2,300	2,200	2,700
Natural Sciences, Mathematics (16.9%)	12,100	8,000	13,400	12,000
Engineering (19.0%)	10,000	3,400	5,100	7,200
Medicine (including 30% of university clinics) (6.3%)	36,800	—	—	36,400
Agricultural Sciences (2.2%)	13,900	8,900	8,300	12,800
Fine Arts (5.0%)	1,500	3,100	2,300	4,800
Total (including central expenditure of institutions)	13,600	11,700	6,900	12,400

the annual budget of the Land passed by its parliament. The Land budget shows incomes and expenditures of the institutions of higher education. Up to the beginning of the seventies, when tuition fees were generally abolished, tuition comprised only a small part of the income, generally lower than one-tenth of the expenditure on research and teaching.[8]

The most significant sources of income of the institutions are their services, especially medical service in the university hospitals, and research commissions. Yet this income only covers a small part of the expenditure of the institutions—(13 percent in 1973).[9] Current expenditures on institutions of higher education are essentially paid for by budgetary provision by the Land.

With regard to research in higher education, the funds budgeted by the Länder for the individual institutions are significantly increased by public funds provided by Bund and Länder and funds from third parties. The most significant agency for additional research funding is the Deutsche Forschungsgemeinschaft. Every academic may apply to the Forschungsgemeinschaft for funds for specific research projects. The Forschungsgemeinschaft also promotes, through special programs, concentration of research in specific areas.

As explained earlier in connection with the functions of the Planning Committee for Construction in Higher Education, the investments of the Land for construction in higher education are supplemented by subsidies of the Bund (50 percent). Furthermore, the Bund participates in investments for student residences (50 percent) and in financial aid to students (65 percent). Being state institutions, the institutions of higher education have no financial autonomy; rather, their financial management is generally integrated with the budget of the Land.[10] Annual allocations are itemized according to purposes (e.g., staff, equipment, and so forth), and only some extent of reallocation is permitted. This means that the purposes for which funds can be used are largely determined by the legislators. The universities in the Saarland and in Berlin are exceptions. They prepare their own budgetary plan and then receive a global allocation from the Land budget. For the preparation of the annual budget by the Ministry of Culture, the institutions of higher education submit detailed requirements which have been drafted by their administrations and decided upon by their autonomous committees (e.g. the "senate"). The budget requirements are reviewed with the Department for Higher Education at the Ministry of Culture. Both the submitted requirements and the reviews form the basis for the budget proposals submitted by the Ministry of Culture to the state parliament. In a few cases (e.g. in Rhineland Palatinate), the state parliament receives the original proposals of the institutions and the budgetary proposals of the Ministry of Culture in order to make its decisions.

A significant change in the way budget decisions are made concerns the abandonment of direct allocations to individual professors. In the past, if a full professor (*Ordinarius*) was appointed, his personal salary, the allocations for his chair, and the number of staff assigned to him were settled in direct negotiations between the professor and the Ministry of Culture—without the participation of the university administration. If a professor received a call to a chair at another university, his personal budget was, as a rule, further increased by so-called "negotiations to remain." This custom of individual allocation—one of the characteristics of the old university system (*Ordinarienuniversität*)—resulted in an allocation of staff and equipment that was not always in line with an optimal allocation of funds for the needs of teaching and research from an overall viewpoint. It was essentially based on the reputation of the professor, and even if a new person was appointed to the chair, the funds allocated generally remained as fixed items in the budget.

The laws for higher education that have been passed by the Länder in recent years have largely restricted the extent of appointment negotiations, which now mainly concern the personal salary of the professors.[11] When this regulation was introduced, however, the problem arose as to whether the "inherited" funds from earlier negotiations were to be kept.[12] The personal income of professors lies within the salary range predetermined for public service. There is, however, a considerable degree of latitude for the salaries of full professors. In 1977, for example, the gross annual income of a full professor, married, forty years old with two children, may be between DM 65,000 and DM 120,000;

salaries over DM 80,000 are based on special arrangements resulting, usually, from having received several "calls" for appointments or outstanding achievements. A married subprofessorial staff member, thirty years old with two children, receives a gross salary of approximately DM 45,000 per annum.

Once the planning procedures now envisaged are generally applied, the budgetary proposals of the institutions of higher education will be based more and more on the equipment plans of the organizational units (departments) and on the institutional development plans. This will ensure a sounder basis on which to construct convincing arguments for the Ministry of Culture.

The university budgets which are integrated in the state budgets are administered according to a fiscal principle in which only receipts and expenditures must be accounted for. Proper bookkeeping is verified by the state auditing office. This guarantees a correct administration of the budget. It is, however, more and more doubtful whether this also ensures not only a correct, but also an economic administration of the budget and an efficient utilization of public funds. More and more demands are made to require internal cost-accounting records in the institutions that will ensure efficient utilization of funds.[13]

Admission of Students

One characteristic of the German university has been the freedom qualified students had to enroll at a university of their choice after they had received the secondary school diploma (*Abitur*) qualifying them to be "mature" for university study. In general, universities are considered to be of equal standing. There are no major differences in status among the universities of the Federal Republic as there are in Anglo-Saxon countries. This is the reason why there is no competition among the universities to get the best students by way of entrance examinations, a fact that often amazes foreign observers.[14]

When enrollment increased dramatically, however, most universities reached the limit of their capacity. This meant that the principle of letting every qualified student choose his or her own university had to be restricted. By the middle of the sixties, universities began to reintroduce the *numerus clausus* that had been practiced briefly in the emergency situation immediately after World War II. In the beginning, it was primarily applied in medicine and natural sciences.

The introduction of the *numerus clausus*, and its intensified use after 1970, was strongly opposed by the public, particularly, of course, by the secondary school graduates who were affected by it. In numerous law suits it was argued that the *numerus clausus* was a violation of the right to a free choice of profession and place of study laid down in the Basic Law (Article 12). The *numerus clausus* and the problems of selection and distribution connected with it have become one of the most critical points in German higher education. In recent years, it has engendered countless state regulations, parliamentary inquiries, legal proceedings, and decisions. A bibliography for the period 1970–76 lists 619 items of this kind, as well as sixty-nine monographs and 460 articles in journals, collective publications, and weeklies dealing with the *numerus clausus* problem.[15]

The basis for future admission policies is the so-called *numerus clausus* verdict of the Federal Constitutional Court in 1972. It expressly underscores the basic right for a free choice of profession and place of study, and states that an absolute *numerus clausus* for new students is only constitutional:[16]

— if it is kept within absolutely necessary limits and if the existing educational capacities supported by public means are utilized to their maximum;
— if appropriate criteria are applied to select students and to assign them to specific universities so that every qualified applicant has a chance and his personal choice of university may be considered.

In order to comply with these principles, the Länder drafted a "state contract for the placement of students" in 1972. On the basis of this contract, a central agency for student placement (Zentralstelle für die Vergabe von Studienplätzen—ZVS) was established.[17] It replaced the central registration agency of the West German Conference of Rectors formed in 1967 which had rendered technical assistance to the institutions of higher education in the placement of students.

The first requirement of the Federal Constitutional Court—ascertaining capacities as the basis for admission regulations—was complied with when regulations to determine capacities were issued in connection with the state contract. This consequence from the ruling of the Federal Constitutional Court has had an extraordinary effect on higher education in the Federal Republic. The highly debated capacity regulations are the first attempt to survey the existing educational capacities in the institutions of higher education of the eleven Länder by applying uniform standards. In contrast to nationwide planning of the system of higher education which is concerned with the provision of space for students, the capacity regulation proceeds primarily from the existing capacity of academic staff; space and equipment capacities are only of secondary concern.

A differentiated, complicated system for the determination of admission capacities was introduced with the capacity regulations of 1974 and 1975.[18] According to these regulations, different values are to be applied to teaching performances by professors, depending on the type of instruction (lecture, seminar, practical courses, thesis supervision, and so forth) and the student-teacher ratio (number of students in any one of the above courses). In the second version of the capacity regulations, no less than thirty different types of instruction were distinguished, about twenty of which related to university instruction. In most Länder—although differences still exist—the teaching load of university professors is eight hours per week. By distinguishing types of instruction, and by assigning value factors from 0.1 to 1.0 to them, a bureaucratic control over the actual provision of teaching was introduced in the history of German higher education. It caused much indignation about government interference, and it probably encouraged much juggling among staff to establish favorable value factors for their teaching performance. The evaluation procedure also resulted in promoting the monologue of the classical one-man lecture, with large student numbers to which the highest value is accorded. The more modern intensive types of instruction with limited numbers have been accorded lower values and therefore have been relegated into the background even though they represent an important element in reform efforts.

In order to avoid the pressure of regimentation by capacity regulations, a number of departments have suggested on their own that they be excluded from the central admission procedure, preferring over-capacity to bureaucratic interference. In the future—also as a result of criticism by the universities—the complicated capacity regulations are to be replaced by broader evaluatory guidelines which once again give more autonomy to the individual institutions as far as the forms of teaching are concerned. However, one cannot know to what extent the new evaluatory guidelines will be an improvement in this respect.

Implementation of the second stipulation of the Federal Constitutional Court, referring to the application of appropriate criteria in admission procedures, is still in its developmental stages. As of now, applicants for *numerus clausus* fields of study are selected by the ZVS by applying "achievement and aptitude" criteria that are based on the grade average of the secondary school diploma (*Abitur*) and on "time of waiting." After deducting special quotas for foreigners and hardship cases, 60 percent of students are admitted according to achievement, and 40 percent according to waiting time. In the most rigorous *numerus clausus* disciplines—particularly medicine— waiting time may be up to six years. Although the ZVS tries to be as accommodating as possible, the applicant must still work his way through a maze of instructions and numerous questionnaires for the ZVS admission procedure. Properly filling-out these forms could in itself be interpreted as proof of the student's "maturity" for university.

There is a general dissatisfaction with the significance ascribed to the grades of the secondary school diploma, which determines to a large extent whether a student can enter a chosen discipline. It also has serious consequences for the secondary schools. Specific criticism is aimed at the fact that individual grades are given a connotation of reliability that they do not possess. It is also charged that competition for one-tenth of a grade poisons the atmosphere in secondary schools. The pressure on secondary school students caused by this situation—although perhaps sometimes exaggerated by the media—is considered by the public to be a special sign of the failure of educational policy.[19]

The Frame Law for Higher Education provides a number of additional regulations for the admission law. The most important of these is the provision that selection for those disciplines requiring a particularly high grade average[20] or especially long waiting periods is to be based on supplementary procedures which include tests and take practical experience into account (HRG Art. 33, paragraph 3). However, such selective tests which are to be introduced for medicine by 1979 are not altogether acceptable. Both experts and officials of the ministries of culture are skeptical as to whether it will be possible to develop testing methods in such a short time.[21] As for the secondary school graduates themselves, they clearly prefer those admission criteria that are relevant to their chosen field—such as aptitude tests and a "probationary semester" with a subsequent examination. Secondary school graduates generally consider the procedures based on grade averages and waiting times, as well as the often acclaimed lottery, to be inadequate.[22]

As long as achievement criteria maintain their significance, the disparities in the requirements at the secondary schools of the eleven Länder pose a special problem for an equitable admission of student applicants. To cope with this problem, another supplementary regulation was included in the Frame Law for Higher Education. It stipulates the establishment of Länder quotas for the selection of student applicants as long as an equivalence of requirements and grading has not been established among the Länder (HRG, Art. 32). The quota of a Land consists of one-third of its applicants and two-thirds of its proportion of eighteen to twenty-one year olds among the population of the Land. The demand for equivalence means that the ministers of culture are forced to standardize requirements for the *Abitur*, a situation that is to be achieved through the introduction of so-called "norm books."[23] These represent a centralistic and rigid intervention in the structure of curricula of secondary schools which in a way contradicts the federal creed of the Conference of Ministers of Culture.

The previous examples only illustrate a small section of the host of problems that arose for the German system of higher education when admission restrictions were introduced. This explains all the more a statement made in the ZVS report:[24]

> In order to abolish the *numerus clausus* as soon as possible, the restriction of the basic right to free choice of profession and place of study (Article 12 of the Basic Right) required in various disciplines must remain the object of criticism by the young people whose life is affected by it, by the public, and by the respective politicians.

In the first years of its existence, the ZVS "only" had to concern itself with ten fields of study restricted by the *numerus clausus*. For the winter semester 1976/77, however, twenty-five fields of study had to be covered by the selective admission procedure because the number of applicants exceeded the available places. At present, extensive efforts are being made with regard to admission policies to relax the *numerus clausus* situation by maximum utilization of facilities and even by admitting more students than the institution could normally accommodate.

According to a resolution of the heads of governments of Bund and Länder in November 1977 "to open up universities," the selection procedure of the ZVS will be limited in the future to a small number of strict *numerus clausus* disciplines for which there is so large a demand that universities would run into severe functional disorder if all applicants were accepted. An overcharge of the available study places by 15 percent has been established as criterion for this. At present and for some time to come this concerns seven courses of study with large numbers of students and five less important disciplines with smaller numbers of students. The strict *numerus clausus* disciplines are medicine, veterinary medicine, dentistry, pharmacy, and psychology in which the number of applicants in recent years was sometimes eight times higher than the places available, as well as biology and architecture. These strict *numerus clausus* fields cover about

15 percent of all study places; in addition, some study courses for teachers are still subject to the selection procedure. The modalities of selection will be revised in the near future by a new state contract between the Länder, to replace that of 1972.

The resolution of November 1977 is an effort to exclude as many study courses as possible from the selection procedure of the ZVS. Some of these continue, of course, to be "bottle-neck fields" with some overcharge. For these, the so-called "local assignment procedure" will still be necessary. However, this refers not to a decision on *whether* the applicant can be admitted at all but only on *where* he can be admitted. At present, eleven "bottle-neck" fields are subject to this procedure including law, economics, and chemistry as well as several study courses in the engineering sciences.[25] This policy strategy to "open up universities," along with growing numbers of student applicants and simultaneous stagnation of personnel capacities, must cause confusion in the public. Critics therefore argue that by this policy "the devil of admission restrictions" is driven out by the "Beelzebub of nonfunctioning universities."[26]

Selection of Faculty

One of the most important duties and privileges of university self-government has always been the right to propose new faculty members for vacant chairs, who are ultimately appointed by the Ministry of Culture of the Land. In the classical tradition of universities, such proposals for the appointment of professors were based on scholarly publications, the applicant's reputation as a scholar, and on informal communications. A prerequisite for an appointment was the *Habilitation*. This means that a scholar who had already obtained a doctorate was granted the *venia legendi*, the qualification to teach in a certain discipline, on the basis of the *Habilitationsschrift*, a scholarly thesis representing an original scientific contribution. In the beginning of the seventies, an important change was made in the appointment procedure: from then on, vacancies were publicly advertised, a procedure that has meanwhile been included in the state laws and is expressly stated in the Frame Law for Higher Education (HRG Art. 45, 1). A *Habilitation* is no longer imperative for an appointment, according to the frame law it can be substituted by equivalent academic contributions or even by outstanding professional achievements (HRG Art. 44). The main reason for this development was the expansion of academic staff in the sixties. It was introduced by the Godesberg recommendation of the West German Conference of Rectors of 1968 for the reform of faculty and personnel structure, and by the statements of the Federal Conference of University Assistants. Their conclusions were:[27]

> that admission to the position as university professor should no longer depend on a *Habilitation* and a "call" for appointment, but that a university career should start out from a doctoral degree and an application for appointment.

In reality, the *Habilitation* is still considered important at many universities. In view of the present stagnation in the number of academic staff, it may once again become more important.

Depending on the state laws, the appointment procedures sometimes differ with regard to details, but there are general guidelines which are followed everywhere. The university forms an appointment committee to draw up a list of proposals; the committee consists mainly of representatives of the particular field for which a vacancy is to be filled. The composition of the appointment committee as to the distinct groups of university members differs according to state laws and university constitutions. As a rule, at least one representative from the subprofessorial staff and one student representative participate in the decisions. No matter how many representatives from these other groups participate, however, their numbers are limited by the 1973 ruling of the Federal Constitutional Court which states that professors must have an absolute majority in all decision-making committees concerning instruction and research. The appointment committee selects from the applications three candidates. Sometimes it is customary to invite the applicants on the select list to give a trial lecture.

The appointment committee must give specific reasons for its proposal of candidates to the university for its decision-making process and to the Ministry of Culture. For the three candidates on the select list a detailed recommendation (*Laudatio*) is written, which covers the candidate's professional career, scholarly achievements, as well as personal and professional qualifications for the advertised position. In addition, some state laws require an evaluation by scholars from other universities. The proposal must state the entire number of applicants, and it must justify the order of preference with regard to the three candidates.

For the appointment, the Ministry of Culture is not bound by the order of preference. It may refuse to consider the list with the three candidates altogether and may ask for a new list. This happens, for example, when negotiations with the candidate selected from the list by the Ministry of Culture fail, and in recent years it has also happened in cases where the political views of the candidate were not acceptable to the ministry. Moreover, legal regulations generally specify that the Ministry of Culture may in exceptional cases and after consultation with the university appoint qualified persons on its own.

According to the frame law, which aims at a standardization of staff structure in higher education, the subprofessional academic staff is to consist of assistants, academic employees, and teaching staff for special functions (HRG § 42 ff). The position of assistant is reserved for those aiming to qualify for a professorship. Their number is, therefore, to be restricted so that there will be a fair chance for an appointment as professor later on. The entry qualification for an assistant is generally the doctorate. Assistants are mostly independent in their research and teaching functions and are obliged to complete an *Habilitation*. Their term of appointment is usually limited to six, or at most eight years. Academic employees, who are to fulfill service tasks in research and teaching may, in contrast, be hired on a long-term basis. The same is true of teaching staff with special functions, who hold positions which are primarily directed to the transmission of practical abilities.

The recruitment of the subprofessional staff, is largely the responsibility of the university itself. Unless these positions can be filled by graduating students of the university or through informal communication, they, too, are often advertised. This is not obligatory however. Recently, if applicants were members of radical political groups, the Ministry of Culture frequently intervened in the hiring procedure in order to investigate whether there might be any constitutional objections to disqualify an applicant for public service.

Development and Change in Curriculum

In the past, the teaching units at universities were almost exclusively responsible for the form and content of instruction. Limitations for such latitude were set by examination regulations. Only a relatively small number of professions—albeit with considerable student numbers such as medicine, teaching, and law—require a state examination for which the government determines the requirements on behalf of the public and in which a government representative participates. However, even the rules for a final university-degree examination—like a master of arts degree or a diploma—must be approved by the Ministry of Culture of the Land.

When reform movements became prominent in the late sixties, a lively discussion began over the organization of curricula in which professors, assistants, and students joined. The specific question was how to maintain and reform the venerable principle of "education through research" in mass education. This discussion received a special impetus from the Federal Conference of University Assistants (Bundesassistentenkonferenz—BAK) which developed the concept of "learning by inquiry" and thus contributed significantly to the discussion of curriculum reforms.[28] The dissatisfaction of the students with existing programs of study led in some cases, for instance at the Free University of Berlin, to the establishment of alternative courses of study which came to be known as "critical universities." With the assistance of the cultural ministries, many universities organized didactic centers to assist in reforming curricula both in form and in substance. There has, however, been a certain disillusionment on the part of the government because the didactic centers at the universities frequently concentrated on basic and critical analyses of university affairs without effecting any practical results for new curricula that would ensure more efficient, shorter, and more concise courses of study.

Since 1968 the Conference of Ministers of Culture, in cooperation with the WRK and with the assistance of the national associations of faculties of individual disciplines, has worked out general rules and principles which were a basis in the reformulation of regulations for state and university examinations. However, this did not solve one of the basic problems of current higher education: overlong periods of study. On the average, students in the humanities, social sciences, natural sciences, and engineering extend their stay at the university by two years beyond the prescribed minimum length of studies. According to the Frame Law for Higher Education, the minimum length of study is to become the prescribed length of study in the future.

In order to tackle this problem, the Frame Law for Higher Education stipulates "study reform commissions" to be formed by the Länder in cooperation with the universities and then to be combined into systemwide study reform commissions. According to the law, the proposed study reform commissions are to include the representatives from institutions of higher education, from the government, and from the individual professions. Among other things, it will be the task of the study reform commissions to make recommendations for:[29]

> the consequences which the development and changes in the sciences and professional activities may have on the goals and substance of courses of study.

These recommendations are to take the form of guidelines. The guidelines must be accompanied by examples of study courses and of examination rules containing specific suggestions for the implementation of the guidelines. The responsible government agency will have the right to demand that courses of study be adapted to the recommendations, or even to issue new study and examination rules.

At present, the Conference of Ministers of Culture is engaged in the creation of systemwide study reform commissions. First priority will be given to establishing commissions for study courses in dentistry, economics, chemistry, mechanical engineering, electrical engineering, social work, and pedagogy. For study courses ending with an academic examination, it is proposed that university representatives will have a simple majority in the commissions, while government representatives will have a two-thirds majority in those dealing with study courses ending with state-board examinations. A permanent commission for study reform will be established in the secretariat of the Conference of Ministers of Culture for the coordination of the study reform commissions. It is to consist of eleven representatives of higher education and eleven representatives of the Länder and—in an advisory capacity—two representatives of the Bund and one representative from each of the employers' association and from the trade unions. Another coordinating committee is envisaged to consist of four representatives both of higher education and the Länder and one representative from the Bund.

It is difficult to say at this point how quickly the study reform commissions can become effective. There is, however, no doubt that, through these commissions, the ministries of culture will gain considerable influence over the determination of curricula in higher education and not only, as until now, on examination regulations and the broad outline of programs of study. The universities consider this to be an infringement on their autonomy and their traditional responsibilities. It is expected that the possibility of government intervention in internal university affairs may become a particular source of conflict between institutions of the higher education sector and the government.

Establishment of New Institutions

During the phase of reconstruction, which lasted until the end of the fifties, the Länder directed their efforts in higher education toward intensified expansion of existing universities in order to be able to absorb the growing number of students. Not until 1960 did they begin to realize that the then thirty-one universities and technical universities could not be expanded *ad infinitum*, but that it would be necessary to establish new institutions of higher education. The main impulse came from the Science Council which in 1960 also proposed the establishment of new institutions in its "recommendations for the expansion of scientific facilities." Initially, it suggested only three universities, one technical university, and special medical colleges.[30]

Responding to the needs of the time, the main objective of the recommendations to establish new institutions was a desire to decrease the pressure on the existing universities. Shortly before the Science Council issued its proposal, the North Rhine Westphalia parliament had already resolved to begin planning of a new university at Bochum in order to disburden their overcrowded state universities (Bonn, Cologne and Münster, as well as the technical university at Aachen). Soon, however, considerations other than the disburdening of old universities became just as important. It was hoped that the building of new universities "from scratch" would open up new opportunities for innovatory approaches to university structure, organization, courses of study, and administration.[31]

The suggestions submitted by the Science Council on the organization of new institutions[32] engendered lively discussions at the university level, especially among student groups.[33]

The recommendation to build new institutions was actively taken up by the Länder; they actually went beyond the extent suggested. In the sixties, more than ten new universities were founded. The first of which, especially have made an effort to combine the traditional idea of a university with the necessary reforms required by changing social conditions. As far as their formation is concerned, the new universities have much in common. Since they are public institutions, they are all based on a parliamentary resolution of the Land prepared by the individual state government. Parallel to the planning concepts of the Land and the systemwide science committees, there was often considerable activity on the part of municipalities. Many cities hoped to be selected for the location of the new institutions.

This is an opportunity to have their infrastructure improved, to create new jobs, and to develop their cultural life. In general, cities view a university as an enhancement both of their economic condition and of their prestige if they can call themselves "university city." Hence, especially in the period that lasted until the beginning of the seventies when a number of new university locations were selected, the cities submitted extensive memoranda and promising offers to the Länder in order to be chosen as the site of a university.

The Länder differed in their initial planning procedures. The creation of new universities in Bavaria and Baden-Württemberg was preceded by comprehensive government memoranda containing both general ideas and considerations of concrete requirements for planning.[34] The first, though never realized plan for the University of Bremen, as well as the general plan for the University of Bielefeld was based on the opinion of individual experts.[35] Besides this preliminary work, the state government generally established a founding committee with advisory functions for each proposed university. In the case of the early universities (Bochum, Dortmund, Konstanz, Ulm, Bielefeld, Regensburg), this committee was an honorary committee consisting essentially of distinguished academics, and its task was to outline the structure for the new university. In this, the founding committee of the University of Konstanz, especially, followed the suggestions of the Science Council on the organization of new universities through a model university which was to be established only in one place and was to have only a limited number of disciplines (natural sciences, humanities, and social sciences).[36]

Of the funds for these new universities of the first phase, which would have exceeded the financial resources of a Land, 75 percent were provided by the investment fund for new institutions of higher education (with the exception of Ulm) which the Länder had set up in 1964 through their "Agreement on the Financing of New Institutions of Higher Education" and in which the Bund was not yet involved.

Since 1970 the founding of new institutions has entered a second stage. The 1970 organizational recommendations of the Science Council, and the ideas contained in the federal "Educational Report 1970" and in the federal-state comprehensive educational plan—both of which are based on the Science Council's 1970 recommendations—now center on the concept of a comprehensive university as the object of further deliberations on university expansion. According to these views, no more "universities" are to be created; rather, new institutions are to be planned and set up as comprehensive institutions of higher education which may sometimes be organized around already existing, smaller institutions like teachers colleges and technical colleges (for a detailed description of comprehensive institutions, see Chapter 5). The Science Council based its 1970 deliberations on the assumption that thirty new comprehensive institutions would be required. Today, this figure seems unrealistic in view of the reduction in expansion. As far as the actual procedure in the planning of comprehensive institutions is concerned, it is characterized by a greater degree of pragmatism than were the new institutions of the first phase with their idealistic planning concepts.[37]

> Until now, it has been the main task of the founding committees for new institutions to work out reform plans. However, future construction of so many new institutions requires not so much a continuing development of innovating plans for institutions, but rather an accelerated realization of models that are suitable for new development.

In line with the recommendations of the Science Council, there are now indications that the parliamentary decision to establish such institutions will no longer be based on voluminous foundation memoranda, but rather on administrative decisions by the ministries of culture. Following the creation of the University of Trier-Kaiserslautern[38] and the Comprehensive University of Kassel, the parliament of North Rhine Westphalia took the most important step so far in the second phase of the creation of new institutions by passing the Law for the Establishment and Development of Comprehensive Institutions of Higher Education in the State of North Rhine Westphalia. Through this law, five new comprehensive institutions were created at one stroke in Duisburg, Essen, Paderborn, Siegen, and Wuppertal. The original institutions of each of these five new establishments were a *Fachhochschule* and a teachers college. They are now under the same roof. By adding university-type courses of study, they partly carry on with their original programs and partly offer new, integrated programs.

Further implementation of the plan is the responsibility of the founding senate which is composed of representatives from all groups—including professors, assistants, and students—of the existing institutions, and of scholars and scientists appointed by the Ministry of Culture for the additional university-type programs.[39] All institutions founded since 1970 have generally turned away from committees consisting only of professors to founding committees of a mixed composition. Still, there are considerable differences with regard to at what point in the process they were established, their tasks, and their effectiveness vis-á-vis administrative directives and the decision-making power of the ministries of culture.[40]

The second phase of the formation of institutions of higher education is not only characterized by a different concept, but also by a different method of financing. According to the common task for construction in higher education, the Bund provides half the funds the Land needs for expansion or new construction of institutions. New institutions require a resolution by the Planning Committee for Construction in Higher Education which in turn is preceded by a vote of the Science Council. This means that the decision to create new institutions, if these are partly to be funded by the Bund, is no longer a matter of state government and state parliament alone. In reality, however, experience so far shows that the planning decisions of the individual Länder mostly represent a *fait accompli* for which agreement is generally not withheld.

With the projects submitted by the Länder for the seventh frame plan for university construction, about 96 percent of the long-term target of study facilities in higher education has been met. This means that the phase of creating "genuinely" new institutions has for the moment come to an end. Future institutions will be created by reorganizing and consolidated existing institutions into comprehensive institutions. Certainly, this process will test the relationship between the government and the universities: the critical point will be whether the ministries of culture act alone or in cooperation with the institutions in question, leaving them as much autonomy as possible.[41]

FOOTNOTES

1. Federal Ministry of Education and Science, *Bildungsbericht '70* (Bonn: 1970), p. 144.
2. Cf. Hesse Ministry of Culture, *Diskussionsgrundlage zur Entwicklungsplanung 1977/78 für die hessischen Hochschulen* (Wiesbaden: 1977), p. 326.
3. See Appendix A for data.
4. Cf. OECD, *Reviews of National Policies for Education: Germany* (Paris: 1972), p. 114.
5. *Ibid.*, p. 114.
6. Federal Ministry of Education and Science, *Grund- und Strukturdaten 1976* (Bonn: 1976), pp. 122-23. Expenditures on higher education do not contain that for financial aid to students. Investments in real assets include investments in buildings, including acquisition of land and original equipment of buildings—as acquisitions of furnishings.
7. Cf. Federal Ministry of Education and Science, *Grund- und Strukturdaten 1977* (Bonn: 1977), pp. 81 and 99. This refers to expenditure on teaching, research and services. Thus, also expenditure on research is included in this calculation which only indirectly pertains to the education of students.
8. Cf. Willi Albert and Christoph Oehler, *Materialien zur Entwicklung der Hochschulen 1950–1967*, HIS Series Hochschulforschung, Volume 1 (Hannover: 1969), p. 400.
9. Cf. Heinz Bolsenkötter (Wibera Project Group), *Ökonomie der Hochschule*, Eine betriebswirtschaftliche Untersuchung (Baden-Baden: Nomos Verlagsgesellschaft, 1976), p. 499.
10. For a discussion of questions and development trends in the funding of higher education cf. Thomas Oppermann, "Hochschulfinanzierung—Status, Tendenzen und Chancen," *Wissenschaftsrecht, Wissenschaftsverwaltung, Wissenschaftsförderung* Volume II (1969), No. 1. Jürgen Fischer, Jens Hoffer, and Helmuth Rose, *Zur Strategie der Finanzplanung im Hochschulbereich* (Köln: Carl Heymanns Verlag, 1973).
11. Also according to the Frame Law for Higher Education (Article 45,

paragraph 4), in future promises of equipment for a new professor may not exceed the amount specified in the equipment plan of the organizational unit in question.
12. Cf. Gerd Roellecke, "Berufungsvereinbarungen und Organisationsgewalt," *Wissenschaftsrecht, Wissenschaftsverwaltung, Wissenschaftsförderung,* Volume IX (1976), No. 1.
13. Cf. e.g. Heinz Bolsenkötter, *op. cit.*, (Footnote 9), p. 475 ff; Jürgen Fischer, Christoph Oehler, and Jürgen Pohle, *Hochschulentwicklungsplanung,* HIS Letter 57 (Munich: Verlag Dokumentation, 1975), pp. 200 ff.
14. For example, the comments of the International Council on the Future of the Universities, which recently visited German universities. The following statement is of course, perfectly justified: "Clearly, the problem of admission is in a state of great confusion at the present time ..." However, it then continued: "But certainly in any pluralistic system of higher education, it would seem fair that universities be permitted to compete for the best students they can get, and to have the authority to select students on the basis of suitability to their special programmes and offerings." (*The Times Higher Education Supplement* June 24, 1977, p. 13). This comment has no real validity for the German system of higher education because it cannot be called "pluralistic" in the Anglo-Saxon sense of the word.
15. Cf. Deutsches Institut für Pädagogische Forschung, ed., *Numerus Clausus Eine Bibliographie,* compiled by Annemarie Schaffernicht (Frankfurt/M.: 1976).
16. West German Conference of Rectors, *Numerus clausus Urteile des Bundesverfassungsgerichts vom 16. Juli 1972 und 9. Februar 1977,* Dokumente zur Hochschulreform XXIX/1977 (Bonn-Bad Godesberg: 1977), p. 43.
17. For details on the legal foundation, the tasks and procedures of the ZVS cf. *Bericht der Zentralstelle für die Vergabe von Studienplätzen, 1973–74,* Dortmund. Cf. also Zentralstelle für die Vergabe von Studienplätzen, *Zweiter Bericht mit Materialien zu den Vergabeverfahren 1974–76,* Dortmund.
18. Cf. *ibid.*
19. Cf. on this question, as well as the present state of discussions about the problems connected with the *numerus clausus* in general, Andreas Flitner, ed., *Der Numerus clausus und seine Folgen* (Stuttgart: Klett, 1976).
20. The required grade average for the *numerus clausus* disciplines in the summer semester of 1976 ranged from 1.7 for medicine, psychology, and biology, to 3.7 for business administration. (*Translator's note:* German grades range from 1, as the highest, to 6, as the lowest grade.)
21. Cf. the article "N-C Test: Countdown ins Ungewisse," *Der Spiegel,* Volume XXXI, No. 7 (February 7, 1977). This article contains a few

indications of the questions in the test for medicine that is in preparation.
22. Cf. Forschungsgruppe Hochschulsozialisation, *Abiturientenuntersuchung 1976*, Preliminary Report (Konstanz: 1976), pp. 59 ff.
23. Cf. on this point Dieter Lenzen, "Die Illusion der Vereinheitlichung— Normenbücher zwischen Testpsychologie und Verfassungsrecht" in Andreas Flitner, *op. cit.*, pp. 37 ff.
24. Zentralstelle für die Vergabe von Studienplätzen, *Zweiter Bericht, op. cit.*
25. Cf. Federal Ministry for Education and Science, *Informationen*, November 1977.
26. Cf. Hermann Avenarius in Andreas Flitner, *op. cit.*, p. 137. One of the critics is the WRK which expects heavy overcrowding in certain areas and institutions because some programs have been excluded from the ZVS procedure. Cf. West German Conference of Rectors, *Arbeitsbericht 1976* (Bonn-Bad Godesberg: 1977), p. 189.
27. Jürgen Fischer, "Kein Platz für Gelehrte," Neue Sammlung, Volume XI, No. 1 (1971), p. 6.
28. Cf. Federal Conference of University Assistants, *Forschendes Lernen, Wissenschaftliches Prüfen* (Bonn: 1970).
29. Frame Law for Higher Education, Article 9, paragraph 4, 1.
30. Cf. Science Council, *Empfehlungen zum Ausbau der wissenschaftlichen Einrichtungen, Part I, Wissenschaftliche Hochschulen* (Bonn: 1960), p. 55.
31. Cf. on this point Hubert Raupach and Bruno W. Reimann, *Hochschulreform durch Neugründungen, Zu Struktur und Wandel der Universitäten Bochum, Regensburg, Bielefeld* (Bonn-Bad Godesberg: Verlag Neue Gesellschaft, 1974); also Eberhard Böning and K. Roeloffs, *Three German Universities, Aachen, Bochum, Konstanz*, Case Studies on Innovation in Higher Education (OECD: Paris, 1970).
32. Cf. Science Council, *Anregungen zur Gestalt neuer Hochschulen* (Bonn: 1962).
33. Cf. on this point, for example, *Studenten und die neue Universität*, Gutachten einer Kommission des Verbandes deutscher Studentenschaften zur Neugründung von wissenschaftlichen Hochschulen (Bonn: 1962); Verband deutscher Studentenschaften, ed., *Studenten an neuen Universitäten*, Eine Schrift zum VII, deutschen Studententag, Bochung, April 23 to 27 (Bonn); also the extensive bibliography in Rolf Neuhaus, ed., *Dokumente zur Gründung neuer Hochschulen* (Wiesbaden: Franz Steiner Verlag, 1968).
34. Reprinted in Rolf Neuhaus, *ibid*.
35. Cf. for Bremen Hans Werner Rothe, "Über die Gründung einer Universität zu Bremen. Denkschrift vorgelegt der Universitätskommission des Senats der Freien Hansestadt Bremen (1960)" in Neuhaus, *ibid.*; for Bielefeld cf. Paul Mikat, Helmut Schelsky, *Grundzüge einer neuen Universität* (Gütersloh: Bertelsmann, 1966).

36. Cf. Die Universität Konstanz. Bericht des Gründungsausschusses (1965), in Neuhaus, *ibid.*
37. Science Council, *Empfehlungen zur Struktur und zum Ausbau des Bildungswesens im Hochschulbereich nach 1970,* Volume I (Bonn: 1970), p. 191.
38. For the history of foundation cf. *Universitätsgründung Trier-Kaiserslautern,* Eine Dokumentation, Issued by the Ministry of Education and Culture, on request of the State Government of Rhineland-Palatinate (Neustadt/Weinstrasse: Daniel Meininger, 1971).
39. For the development of comprehensive institutions in North Rhine Westphalia, cf. Ministry of Science and Research of the State of North Rhine Westphalia, *Gesamthochschulen in Nordrhein-Westfalen,* Materialien zu Aufbau Entwicklung und Funktion (Düsseldorf: 1977).
40. Cf. also the detailed analysis on the course of planning for comprehensive institutions of higher education in paragraph 4.2 of the article by Peter Müller, "Integrierte Gesamthochschule oder differenzierte Gesamthochschulplanung," *Studentische Politik,* Volume 8, No. 1/2 (1975), pp. 179 ff.
41. Cf. e.g. the documentation on the preparation of an integrated comprehensive institution in Hamburg by Harro Plander, "Gesamthochschule im Werden—Kritisches Resümee bisheriger Entwicklungen in Hamburg," in Karl-Heinz Flechsig, Ludwig Huber, and Harro Plander, *Gesamthochschule—Mittel oder Ersatz für Hochschulreform?* (Stuttgart: Klett, 1975), pp. 94–143.

III
EFFECTIVENESS OF HIGHER EDUCATION

INTRODUCTION

In its transition from education for the elite to education of the masses, the system of higher education in the Federal Republic is undergoing a thorough change. This process has far-reaching consequences for the system of higher education itself, and for the relationship between institutions of higher education and society.

The effectiveness of the system of higher education will be put to the test in this situation and it must prove that it can adjust to new demands. For a long time, the institutions have reacted to expansion only insofar as they have accepted, more or less readily, the influx of students; the transition from elite to mass education was not accompanied by appropriate structural changes. Meanwhile, as the *numerus clausus* indicates, the capacity of the traditional system to absorb increasing numbers of students has been nearly exhausted. Hence, the 1976 interim statement on educational policy by the Federal Ministry of Education and Science is of special relevance to the system of higher education: "In the past years, the available educational facilities have essentially been expanded within traditional structures. Organization and substance have not been changed in accordance with needs."*

Transformation of the system of higher education takes place within the framework of social structures and objectives. The expansion of the tertiary level was achieved, mainly, by the demand for university graduates in the sixties and, later, by the movement towards the goal of a "civil right to education." However, the academic labor market, perhaps more so than the sys-

---

* Federal Ministry of Education and Science, *Bildungspolitische Zwischenbilanz* (Bonn: 1976), p. 30.

tem of higher education, evolved within traditional structures. As a consequence, the expansion of the system of higher education has meanwhile surpassed the capacity of the labor market to absorb university graduates. The rigidity of this market in turn affects the system of higher education and hampers its adjustment rather than supports it.

In the following sections we shall, first of all, describe the concepts and innovative measures in the changing system of higher education (see Chapter 5). Subsequently, we shall show what this changing system does for society: Does it measure up to the demand for highly qualified professionals? To what degree does it comply with the educational demands of individuals and yet ensure equal educational opportunity for all? What is the role of research within an institution, and in which way does it contribute to the solution of social problems? (Chapter 6) Finally, we shall point to structural connections within the system of higher education that will specifically determine its future efficiency (Chapter 7).

5 INNOVATION AND FLEXIBILITY

Structural Reform

The concept of a comprehensive institution of higher education is one answer to the changing needs of the tertiary level. This concept was first developed and presented to the public in Baden-Württemberg toward the end of the sixties. It has since been further elaborated in numerous drafts and plans. In a comprehensive institution of higher education, institutions with different functions are consolidated. The comprehensive institution is supposed to form the frame for the future development of higher education that has been agreed upon by the Bund and the Länder in the comprehensive education plan and in the Frame Law for Higher Education.

As we have shown, the present system of higher education consists of institutions with quite different traditions, especially the universities, teachers colleges, and *Fachhochschulen*. The most significant elements are the old universities and the new universities which were founded in the sixties. The universities are oriented toward the classical educational ideal of pure science and research. They are guided by an ideal of academic freedom which gives the students the possibility and responsibility to determine for themselves both what subjects they will take and the duration of their studies. However, when the universities became mass institutions in which personal contact between teachers and students was no longer guaranteed, such academic freedom could result in considerable disorientation. There are signs of such disorientation now—in prolonged periods of study, frequent changes of academic fields, and high drop-out rates. The problem is less serious in medicine in which programs have always been—just as in the areas of technology and natural sciences—relatively more structured. However, the overall lack of curricula orientation prompted the first of the Science Council's recommendations for a study reform in higher education. It proposed a clear structuring of all courses of study so that most students would have four years of study, and medical students six years of study. An additional program would follow for those who qualified to go into research.[1]

The remaining tertiary level institutions have different traditions: the teachers colleges emerged from teachers seminaries, and the *Fachhochschulen* from former engineering schools and other vocational secondary schools (e.g., economics and social work) and their focus was on education for practical purposes. These institutions are regionally more scattered and have far fewer students. In contrast to university studies, the programs at these institutions are more rigidly structured. To use a shorthand, they are more "school-like" than the universities with their ideas of "self-determination and academic freedom." This formula, however, has, for many, a disreputable connotation and has thus been a considerable strain on efforts to reform the structure of higher education.

The deliberations to incorporate the existing institutions into a system of comprehensive institutions were based on several different motivations: to increase the capacity of the system of higher education; to promote transfers among different types of institutions; to extend the traditional research and teaching orientation of the universities to all institutions of higher education; and to achieve greater efficiency by sharing educational facilities. We shall briefly discuss "capacity" and "orientation toward science and research": two questions that have been considered conflicting motivations for the creation of comprehensive institutions.[2]

Capacity

An examination of the classical educational pyramid from elementary school to university reveals a rather atypical trend: on the tertiary level, the pyramid appears to be inverted. The universities, with about three-fifths of all entering students, rest on the rather slim neck of the three-year teachers colleges and *Fachhochschulen,* which have about two-fifths of all entering students. Because students can now transfer more easily, and because of the prolonged duration of studies, the top of this pyramid (representing university education) has swelled into a balloon.

This phenomenon was the basis for the first model of a differentiated comprehensive institution of higher education, the so-called "Dahrendorf Plan" of 1967 drawn up upon the request of the Ministry of Culture of Baden-Württemberg.[3] The Dahrendorf Plan not only proposed an expansion of practice-oriented programs of study at *Fachhochschulen,* but also strongly argued for the introduction of three-year programs at the universities with a concentration on teaching rather than research. Since the number of applicants in higher education was expected to increase, this plan was an attempt to avoid an inversion of the educational pyramid on the tertiary level.

With its 1966 recommendations advocating a division into regular and graduate programs of study, the Science Council had already encroached upon the "sacred cow"—the orientation of study toward research. The Dahrendorf Plan, even more so, aroused violent opposition both among conservative professors and leftist students. It offers a good example of the conflict between upholding research and academic freedom, on the one hand, and complaints that universities are becoming too "school-like" on the other hand.

In 1970, the Science Council also recommended shortened three-year programs for universities.[4] However, after visiting forty-five institutions in 1971, the council realized that the proposal faced heavy opposition. Critics argued that studies would become too "school-like" and that an academic education could not be obtained in three years. Problems connected with the demands of the labor market were also mentioned. Yet these arguments were quite contradictory. On the one hand, there were doubts that the traditional labor market was ready to offer positions to graduates of such programs; on the other hand, there were criticisms that such suggestions were meant only to meet the needs of the labor market and that the graduates of three-year programs would be unprotected against the "exploitations of capitalism" since they lacked flexibility and a broad education.[5]

On account of this rejecting or at least passive attitude of the universities, it was not to be expected that the idea of short programs of study would prevail. In view of the growing number of students, discussion of this idea has been revived. This would result in classifying the sector of university study into three rather than two levels of qualification: short study programs (three years), regular programs (four to five years) and graduate/doctorate programs, for which a ratio of about 50:45:5 has been proposed.[6] However, chances for realizing such a plan do not seem to have improved very much, even now.

Orientation Toward Research and Science

Although they differ in terms of their traditions and ideologies, the institutions of higher education have moved closer together. It had always been true that the universities not only trained future researchers, but also prepared the majority of students for a practical profession. In the traditional system, such training followed after university study in an obligatory period of practice—as in the case of high school teachers, lawyers, and doctors. Today there are more and more demands to acquaint the student with the practical application of his professional knowledge already at the universities. On the other hand, there is also a desire to introduce those who study at the more practice-oriented *Fachhochschulen* to more new scientific methods and knowledge.

These ideas were the point of departure for the democratic-egalitarian concept of an integrated comprehensive institution, the principles of which were developed by the Federal Conference of University Assistants.[7] They proposed to abolish the hierarchy of university diplomas and academic levels. They demanded a reduction in the discrepancy between narrowly theoretical academic programs and the narrowly practical programs of *Fach-*

hochschulen and teachers colleges. This plan, too, included provisions for gradiating diplomas according to various periods of study. However, the initial period of study was to be the same for all fields, without differentiating between short programs concentrating on instruction and long programs relating to research. Restrictions on the period of study were rejected. The Conference of Assistants also demanded that hierarchy of institutions and faculty be abolished and that an integrated system of higher education be created in which every member had an equal opportunity for teaching and research.

These two drafts—the Dahrendorf Plan and the plan of the Federal Conference of University Assistants—delineate the spectrum of plans for comprehensive institutions of higher education as they were developed in the Federal Republic of Germany at the end of the sixties.[8] They have frequently been characterized as being based on conflicting points of view. We believe that such a judgment is too one-sided. The objective of both concepts was to increase the possibilities for access to higher education but in this the emphasis differed. The plan of the Federal Conference of University Assistants envisaged a scientific orientation of all institutions of higher education, while the Dahrendorf Plan proposed a functional division into instruction and research-oriented types of studies. Consolidation through the formation of comprehensive institutions would facilitate transfers and guarantee mutual exchange between the different types.

The initial deliberations by the Bund on the Frame Law for Higher Education were aimed at a model of an administratively integrated comprehensive institution of higher education.[9] The opposition to such a radical change in the system of higher education was especially strong from the Länder with a CDU government. For this reason, the Frame Law for Higher Education now leaves both options—the integrated and the cooperative comprehensive institution—as possibilities for a new system:

> Institutions of higher education are to be organized and consolidated into comprehensive institutions (integrated comprehensive institutions) or to be combined into comprehensive institutions through joint committees, maintain-

ing their legal autonomy (cooperative comprehensive institutions). (HRG Article 5, paragraph 1)

Since, at present, there is a certain weariness with regard to reform plans, the lively debate over the advantage of models for comprehensive institutions has died down. At the present time it cannot be said how far the objective of establishing at least cooperative comprehensive institutions as the general type of higher education will actually be realized. Current developments range from: comprehensive institutions in which the Länder have combined regionally scattered institutions into planning units without making any visible efforts toward cooperation; genuinely cooperative comprehensive institutions with joint programs but different internal structure and hierarchy; and comprehensive institutions founded since 1970 which are based on various integration models. Comprehensive institutions in North Rhine Westphalia, for example, are based on the so-called "Y" model. Comprehensive institutions that follow the "Y" model have two-year integrated primary courses for students and faculty of the various types of institutions. This primary course is followed by programs which are differentiated according to the traditional manner into one-year practically oriented specialized programs and two-year theoretically oriented programs, the choice of which is generally determined by performance in the primary course. Hamburg intends to apply the "consecutive model" according to its preliminary deliberations for the integration of its institutions of higher education. This model calls for a joint three-year program for all students, ending with the first examination that qualifies students for their professions. More examinations are planned after four and six years of study.[10]

In general, the model of a comprehensive institution has lost political support, even though it has only recently been stipulated in the Frame Law for Higher Education as a basis for future development. Apart from the newly established institutions, it is doubtful whether it will be effective as a guideline for the reorganization of the existing system of higher education.[11]

The reform was meant to create interrelated programs of study which were classified according to subject matter and periods of study. This would facilitate transfer from one institution to another and thus improve educational opportunities. It was hoped that by forming comprehensive institutions, the pyramid would be broadened at the tertiary level and the shortened programs would provide places for an increasing number of students.

One of the main reasons for disillusionment with this approach is the fact that students do not seem to be in favor of three-year programs, whereas much larger numbers than expected take advantage of the opportunity to transfer from *Fachhochschulen* to universities. This trend will probably continue as long as the employment market favors graduates of four-year programs over graduates of three-year programs (cf. Chapter 6). On the other hand, the universities have become so overburdened with educational responsibilities that there is little initiative left for reform considerations and for the development of three-year programs, which the universities still see as something foreign.

In view of this situation, in 1975 the chairman of the Science Council revised the 1970 recommendation for comprehensive institutions of higher education which had been one of the origins of the concept of comprehensive institutions included in the Frame Law for Higher Education and in the plans of the Federal-State Commission. Instead, the chairman put forward the concept of an alternative structural model for the system of higher education "in which the comprehensive institution of higher education possibly has an important place, although not the only one."[12] This concept represents a renunciation of the extreme position which would have made comprehensive institutions the basic instrument of extending research-oriented programs of study to the entire system of higher education. The Science Council now advocates a more open, demand-oriented system in which the narrow neck of the lower level of institutions is to be widened:[13]

> If this quantitatively open model is to be continued for a longer period, a sufficient variety of educational opportunities that are institutionally guaranteed must definitely be offered. Depending upon the area and level of study, there should be as small a difference between two adjacent final

examinations as possible. The model definitely cannot open the university for all or even the majority of qualified students. This would be economically impossible, it would be irresponsible toward the students, and it would be highly detrimental to research. Unfortunately, we have already been for too long a time oriented toward universities.

The plans for comprehensive institutions brought new considerations into the discussions of the reform of German higher education—flexibility, transferability, learning by inquiry, and the relation between theory and practice. Although these concepts are innovative, they are still tied to the idea of a closed educational institution that represents a phase of studies between secondary education and profession. To be sure, many plans include possibilities for continuing education for those who are already pursuing their professions (recommendations of the Science Council since 1970, Comprehensive Educational Plan, Educational Report 1970, and so on). However, their implementation has not yet gone beyond the experimental stage.

In addition, proceeding from the concept of the comprehensive institution, proposals have been discussed which exceed existing structures even more radically; they resemble the American concept of a "university without walls." One of these proposals is the plan of a "building-block university." This is intended to give everyone the opportunity to participate in a form of higher education that does not only include training in a discipline, but would, above all, consist of interdisciplinary and problem-oriented study blocks. This would be an all-day program, each block taking about four to six weeks. According to this plan, the instructors would not only be university professors, but also professionals from areas outside the university. Attendance in the individual blocks would be certified. The objective is a flexible and individual organization of studies which generally allows the students to set up their own programs of study from various blocks at different institutions, including extension courses, and thus to be able to make their own decisions on their professional qualifications.[14] Another similar concept is the "sandwich university"[15] which is to enable students to alternate between university studies and practice. The plan presented by Friedrich Edding is the most radical break with the idea that university studies are a limited educational phase following secondary school graduation. Edding's plan is characterized by catchwords like "life-long learning at intervals" and "change of places of learning."[16]

In the scenario of German universities, however, such concepts are not likely to be realized as comprehensive plans. They will meet the stubborn resistance characteristic of a state university system—a system that can hardly be expected to experiment with concepts which are designed not only to reform, but to change the traditional university structures radically. In such cases, one regrets the lack of interplay between state and private institutions. Unhampered by bureaucracy, private institutions would be able to take up and test such possibilities more easily. Even though a nationwide implementation of such plans is not discussed, they still represent "starting points for a change of educational policy thinking," as Edding called his plan, and some elements of these are taken up by individual institutions as instructional experiments.[17]

Innovation in Learning

In the past ten years, parallel and in response to basic discussions of a structural reform of the German system of higher education, a large number of medium-scale innovations have been introduced at the individual institutions of higher education, both with respect to course content and the organization of programs.[18] The maxim established in the Frame Law for Higher Education, that study reform is a continuous responsibility of the institutions of higher education (HRG Article 8), has been accepted by them at least since the end of the sixties.

The study reform received considerable impetus from the student reform movement and from the proposals of the Federal Conference of University Assistants, which were, in part, formed in reaction to the confused conditions existing at the universities and stimulated the introduction of new forms of learning. Further incentives for study reform came from the newly founded universities and from the reorganization of the large old disciplines into smaller departmental units. Departmental units were first introduced at the universities of Bochum and Konstanz and they now represent the lowest level of organizational units at almost all universities. It was much easier to press for development and innovation of curricula on the basis of smaller, more surveyable units than with the large faculties.

Development of Curricula

As we have mentioned, the first results of attempts at study reform are increasing efforts to set up clearer organizational structures for the traditional programs and to make them binding for all universities by establishing study regulations. This is accomplished through interaction between departments and systemwide organizations such as faculty associations, the West German Conference of Rectors, and the ministries of culture. In a recent poll, four-fifths of the university teachers surveyed stated that during the past four years study regulations in their fields had either been issued or changed. The fields which sometimes still lack study regulations are humanities and social sciences. According to their own statements, almost half the teachers in higher education are involved in study reform.[19]

In part, the study reform is also aimed at a general revision and modernization of programs of study, but this is still mostly in the experimental stage. One of these experiments is a pilot project for a single-phased law program which several universities are offering as an experiment until 1981. The purpose of this program is to integrate theoretical studies at the university with the subsequent practical training period in the public judiciary system, and combine both into one program of studies.

The new regulations for medical licensing, as well as the new approach to provide an integrated education of teachers at the University of Oldenburg, are based on similar intentions. Some efforts are also made in natural and engineering sciences to incorporate a certain amount of practical experience and aspects of the social sciences related to later occupations into the programs of study. Frequently, such attempts, however, are not obligatory for the students and not considered necessary by the ministers of culture. The objective of these efforts is to avoid programs that are too theoretically specialized and to counter the danger of creating "specialized idiots" by creating more flexible and critical attitudes on the part of the students toward their future professional activities. The teaching centers that have been established at several universities often serve as focal points for the development of such initiatives.

A third initial step in the direction of curriculum innovations is the creation of completely new programs of study which fill the gaps existing in the available programs. Among these are, for example, interdisciplinary programs for political science and public administration. These programs qualify students for positions in public administration, in associations, and economic enterprises for which until now law graduates had a monopoly although their education cannot be regarded as optimal preparation for the manifold functions and increasing number of positions in the field of public administration. New programs also include those of economic engineers and teachers at vocational schools, as well as pedagogic programs preparing students for the growing field of adult education. The comprehensive institutions that are being established will offer further initiatives to develop innovative programs for new occupations.

New Forms of Learning

Besides the development of course content, the introduction of new methods of learning is also an important aspect of study reform. The provision of teaching is generally dominated by formal lecture courses which offer a systematic survey of the subject, by seminars, by classes, and, particularly in the natural sciences, by practical courses in which special projects are worked out. However, with regard to the "mass" subjects, the possibility of a dialogue between teachers and students in the seminars and classes hardly exists anymore in the large universities because of the large number of students. In general, the German system of higher education does not have a tutorial system as it is practiced in Anglo-Saxon countries.

In recent years, these traditional forms of learning have been supplemented. We should mention the initial steps for programmed learning based on textbooks and scripts, as well as the extension courses promoted by the government. For a long time, little progress was made in developing extension courses because of difficulties of cooperation between Länder and television and radio media, as also because of the lack of interest on the part of the institutions of higher education. In 1977, finally, a broad pilot project was started offering programs in four disciplines.[20] Another important step toward the introduction of extension courses has been made with the foundation of the extension university in Hagen (North Rhine Westphalia). In its third year (1977) more than 10,000 students had already enrolled and a network of about 30 study centers had been set up. In contrast to its original intention it seems, however, that the extension university is predominantly used as an institution for adult education rather than as an alternative for regular study programs at the overcrowded universities.

In many institutions efforts are made to develop forms of teaching and learning that will improve personal and social communication. This is done in work groups and tutorial groups. The incentive for these often comes from the students and has partly been supported by the Volkswagen Foundation. At some institutions, orientation units have been introduced for new students. They render assistance with problems that arise for a student in the transition from secondary schools to the anonymity of a large university.

Several universities are experimenting with intensive courses (*Kompaktkurse*). This is, for instance, the way in which the study of literature is organized at the University of Bielefeld. If such a course is set up only for a single subject, however, there will be problems of coordination. Students who attend all-day intensive courses cannot simultaneously attend the courses in other fields that are organized in the traditional manner—that is, given in two to four hours per week over the entire semester.

This is why intensive courses are generally offered at the beginning or end of the semester when no other courses are given.

The most important and most radical attempt to change the conventional learning procedure is the introduction of so-called "project study." It is based on the following principles:[22]

— The project is developed upon the initiative of groups of students and teachers who are jointly responsible for planning and execution.
— The project concerns practical problems of social relevance that are related to the future occupations. The problem is to be "studied" by taking into consideration the resulting interdisciplinary perspectives and by using as many methods as possible.
— "Project study" is based on learning by inquiry.

Whether these initial attempts of project studies will receive wider application depends to a large extent on the initiative of students and on the readiness of teachers to become involved in such unconventional studies. In the present structural organization of the university, such initiatives often encounter obstacles. How can the performance of a single student be evaluated in a cooperative undertaking? How can the contribution of the teacher be evaluated in terms of his prescribed teaching load? As in the intensive courses, there are further problems relating to coordination with conventional teaching procedures.

Wherever there has been experimentation with project studies, the effort required many compromises. With a few exceptions, project studies have become a marginal and voluntary phenomenon of university life. Only at the newly founded University of Bremen have project studies become the basic organizational principle for studies.[23]

Pilot Projects

As we mentioned, the Pilot Projects in Higher Education, initiated in 1971 by the Federal-State Commission, which we have already pointed out, is an important addition to the diverse attempts at study reform. The first project was introduced in 1971 at the university of Augsburg. It was an experiment with single-phased law studies—the integration of theoretical and practical training of law students. In 1972, twelve pilot projects were funded by the government; their number increased to eighty-four in 1976, and by 1977 there were ninety government-subsidized experiments.

The working group, Pilot Projects in Higher Education, is responsible for the coordination of pilot projects. It is a subgroup of the Committee for Innovations in the Educational System of the Federal-State Commission (BLK). Like the composition of the BLK, it is staffed with representatives of the ministries of culture—eleven delegates of the Länder and two Bund representatives—but no university representatives. Those who are interested in carrying out pilot projects can only submit their suggestions to the respective Ministry of Culture, which will then decide whether to use this suggestion for its own proposal to the BLK. This means that the cultural government agencies have virtually complete control over this reform instrument. The selection of pilot projects is based on the following principles:[24]

— The pilot project must be innovative.
— The pilot project must conform to the objectives and planning of Bund and Länder.
— The pilot project must be designed in such a way as to facilitate decisions that concern the development of the system of higher education.
— The results of a pilot project must be applicable to other areas in higher education.
— A regionally balanced distribution of pilot projects with comparable subjects and of comparable quality is desired.
— Pilot projects are to be planned and implemented by cooperation between government and institutions of higher education.

The pilot projects are supposed to stimulate change and contribute to the reorganization of the system of higher education. In order to accomplish this, a systematic reporting and evaluation procedure has been set up which is also to serve as the working basis for the systemwide study reform commissions. Seven of the thirteen points of concentration of the pilot project program concern aspects of university and study reform in its narrower sense. We shall list each of them along with one example:[25]

- Pilot projects for the planning and development of *comprehensive institutions of higher education* (unless only individual programs are involved), seven projects:
  Example: Model of a comprehensive institution: consolidation of regionally dispersed, heterogeneous institutions where commuting is difficult. Concentration and division of tasks between research and teaching; an attempt is made to bring about integration or cooperation of the individual units. (In the area Ulm/East Württemberg)
- Pilot projects to increase the *efficiency of teaching and learning* also by using the media (including measures to shorten length of studies and residence), eleven projects:
  Example: Chemistry curriculum and multimedia system; development of a chemistry curriculum by means of a multimedia system. The basis is the multimedia system "CHEMS" at the University of California at Berkeley.
- Pilot projects for *extension courses,* five projects:
  Example: Development of long-distance study material, including the production of study letters for mathematics and economics, and the organization of a network of long-distance study centers.
- Pilot projects *to develop graduated programs of study* in disciplines represented in universities and in *Fachhochschulen,* nine projects:
  Example: Integrated programs for architecture and technology; introduction and evaluation of a system of coordinated programs in architecture and technology, particularly architecture, urban and landscape planning, civil engineering, mechanical and electrical engineering (comprehensive institution at Kassel).
- Pilot projects to examine and *further develop existing programs,* nine projects:
  Example: Planning of a basic program of studies for natural sciences: development of a joint basic curriculum for chemistry, physics, and biology.
- Pilot projects to *reform the education of teachers:*
  Example: Development of a standardized means of training of physics teachers: training of physics teachers for intermediate and advanced secondary school years. Students are able to transfer from one program into another. They have the opportunity

to participate in in-service programs. Courses are set up in a building block system.
— Pilot projects for *single-phase studies of law:*
   Example: Integration of practical training into programs of study, including sociological issues.

Reform Under Conditions of Constraint

In the past decade, initiatives for structural and study reforms have resulted in changes and innovations which seem too extensive for many people and too limited for others.

The institutions of higher education of the Federal Republic of Germany have not yet achieved the great breakthrough to a modern system of higher education, although there have been many important first steps toward a reform of both the content and form of studies. These initial steps were worked out at a time when the universities were preoccupied with the reorganization of traditional faculties and their institutes into departments, with the establishment of new constitutions and with what was frequently bitter infighting among various groups within the institutions. In view of this, any attempts for a study reform must be seen as a considerable achievement.

As we outlined earlier, the main challenge to the flexibility of the system of higher education is its ability to offer educational opportunities which meet increasing quantitative demands. This objective, however, has not been reached with the innovations that have been introduced up till now. The study regulations that have been established in almost all disciplines, for example, have actually not led to a shortening of the period of study within a discipline; nor has a reduction of the total length of studies been achieved, it has, quite the contrary considerably increased (see Table 13).[26]

These data refer to the total average length of time which students remain in higher education. They also take account of drop-out students (approximately 13 percent at present), so that the average period for successful completion of higher education is even longer. On the other hand, these figures also cover the

TABLE 13
Average Duration of Residence by Area of Study, 1970–1975
(in years)

Area of Study	1970	1975	Change 1975 versus 1970 (in %)
Total University Disciplines	5.3	6.1	+ 15%
Medicine	6.2	6.5	+ 5%
Mathematics and Natural Sciences	5.0	6.1	+ 22%
Engineering Sciences	5.9	6.7	+ 14%
Humanities (including Teachers Colleges)	4.7	5.4	+ 15%
Law, Economics, and Social Sciences	5.5	6.3	+ 15%
Programs at Fachhochschulen	3.1	3.4	+ 10%

prolongation of study periods caused by students entering a second program of study or by changing the field of study. This has increased considerably since 1970. It is assumed that approximately 20–25 percent of the present student body have changed their fields of study once or even more than once—a pattern which has been promoted by the so-called *Parkstudium* in consequence of the *numerus clausus* admission procedures: according to estimates of the BMBW approximately 50,000 students have in recent years enrolled for an interim period in study programs which did not meet their real interests and professional aims while waiting for being admitted in a *numerus clausus* discipline. This practice has been barred by the new admission regulations as stipulated in the frame law.

In contrast to the total length of study, the average period of study within a discipline has not increased over the last few years. It is, however, still considerably longer than the minimal period required in the study and examination regulations.

In view of this situation the Science Council has made the following statement: "The urgency of a study reform that takes into account the large numbers of students has not been sufficiently and clearly comprehended, and the reform has not been adequately implemented."[27] The need for reform that is quantitatively efficient is considered the key problem for coming years. The guidelines for such a reform are clearly stated in the Frame Law for Higher Education. The Science Council's 1976 recommendations regarding size and structure of the tertiary level deal with this problem in greater detail. Their tenor is a mixture of panic and forceful optimism:[28]

> The time limit we have for the necessary initiatives is so short, and the problems are so manifold, that we cannot simply wait for spontaneous action by professors and students, administrations and the labor market. Planning and legislative measures ... are indispensable.

The most important measures, most of which are in the Frame Law for Higher Education, can be summarized as follows:

— prevention of *Parkstudium* through the reformation of admission regulation in *numerus clausus* disciplines.
— introduction of a fixed time during which studies must be completed;
— introduction of more three-year programs not only at *Fachhochschulen* but also at the universities;
— promotion of independent studies and more intensive use of extension and media teaching which do not involve face-to-face contact;
— formation of study reform commisions whose task is not only to reduce the content of present courses of study, but also to revise course content and adjust courses to the needs of new areas of employment, as well as to add shorter programs to those that are presently offered;
— introduction of obligatory student counseling in order to create a better foundation for the students' choice of studies and to minimize change of fields.
— restriction of opportunities to undertake a second academic education.

Many of these demands were already included in the Science Council's 1970 recommendations; since then, they have often been reiterated by various planning agencies, although no decisive progress has been made. Others, such as the restrictions on opportunities for a second academic education, are a regrettable consequence of the existing crisis. It remains to be seen whether the legal rules can be enforced before the number of students has reached its peak in 1985.

The reduction of periods of study can be considered one of the most important reform measures. The comprehensive educational plan (BGPL) already listed target values that assumed a considerable reduction of the period of study, particularly at universities. This is illustrated in Table 14.[29]

TABLE 14
Average Duration of Study by Area of Study, 1975 and 1985
(in years)

Area of Study	1975 Real Values	1985 BGPL Values	1985/75 Decrease in %
Total University Disciplines	6.1	4.5	— 26%
Medicine	6.5	6.5	0
Mathematics and Natural Sciences	6.1	4.2	— 31%
Engineering Sciences	6.7	4.5	— 33%
Humanities	5.4	4.0	— 26%
Law, Economics, and Social Sciences	6.3	4.5	— 29%
Programs at *Fachhochschulen*	3.4	3.1	— 9%

If the government measures are to have even a chance of being effective in time for future student growth, the universities must be ready to cooperate and react flexibly. There are indications of such a reaction in instances when professors are expected to help master the mounting problems of increased enrollment. A case in point is the professors' general willingness to accept the temporary emergency measures with regard to teaching loads mentioned earlier. If it is a matter of interference with the basic autonomy of the university—the organization of instruction—no such reaction can be detected. We have previously outlined the scope of conflicts that might arise when the study reform commisions become effective (cf. Chapter 4).

The universities are not only skeptical about the organizational aspects of study reform commissions by which reform is to be pushed forward under conditions of increased constraint; their skepticism also relates to those aspects of university reform that concern course content. Indeed, according to the previously mentioned poll in the winter semester 1976/77, teachers in higher education generally believe that courses of study still require a revision of content; they doubt, however, that it is possible to cut back on courses to the extent that the legislators have asked that study reform commissions to do. A great number of teachers (68 percent) believe that the present minimal periods of study will hardly enable the average student to complete his studies in accordance with present study and examination regulations. It may therefore be assumed that university teachers will side with the students in rejecting strict adherence to a fixed time of study. A majority of the teachers (75 percent) also deny that most programs can easily be cut by one year. They believe that shortened programs will result in a further conversion of university study into "school-like" study, a trend that universities, as we know, regard with displeasure. University teachers are also often skeptical about extension courses that are at present being offered (58 percent).[30]

This poll clearly indicates that cooperation between government and higher education will be seriously tested in further implementation of study reform. The attitude of the universities is characterized by fears "that along with the old university's easily recognizable faults its less obvious advantages will be eliminated as well—what Habermas has called 'the remnants of those agreeably archaic freedoms.' "[31] These offered students the liberty to determine for themselves how long and what subjects they would study.

The general trend in the Federal Republic of Germany, however, seems to be towards an adaptation of the Anglo-Saxon system in which university education for most student consists of a curriculum, that is largely laid down and structured, followed by programs of more independent advanced studies for few qualified students. In this context, it remains an open question whether the plan to introduce three years programs of study side by side with the regular four-year programs in the universities can be realized. It is also unclear whether the long-standing plans for recurrent education can be implemented in the near future in view of the student "boom" expected for the next decade.

Prerequisites for a stronger regimentation of the normal curriculum, such as, for example, the continuous counseling that is being tried out now in pilot projects, have not progressed very far. Another unsolved problem is the integration of unconventional and varied concepts of study, of which there are some positive examples, into the new-style curriculum. They conflict with the interests of the ministries of culture which, in view of the crisis management necessary for the coming years, want to establish clear and comparable regulations for institutions of higher education. This is one of the many growth pains that occur in the transition from elitist to mass higher education.

FOOTNOTES

1. Cf. Science Council, *Empfehlungen zur Neuordnung an den wissenschaftlichen Hochschulen* (Bonn: 1966).
2. Cf. for example Ulrich Teichler, "Problems of West German Universities on the Way to Mass Higher Education," *Western European Education*, Volume VIII, Nos. 1–2, (1976), p. 98.
3. Cf. Ministry of Culture of Baden-Württemberg, ed., *Hochschulgesamtplan Baden-Württemberg* ("Dahrendorf-Plan"), Empfehlungen zur Reform von Struktur und Organisation der Wissenschaftlichen Hochschulen, Pädagogischen Hochschulen, Studienseminare, Kunsthochschulen, Ingenieurschulen und Höheren Fachschulen. Bericht des Arbeitskreises Hochschulgesamtplan beim Kultusministerium Baden-Württemberg, Bildung in neuer Sicht, Series A, No. 5 (Villingen: Neckar Verlag, 1967).
4. Cf. Science Council, *Empfehlungen zur Struktur und zum Ausbau des Bildungswesens im Hochschulbereich nach 1970* (Bonn: 1970), p. 19.
5. Cf. Science Council, "Bericht über die Hochschulbesuche im Sommersemster 1971," *Empfehlungen und Stellungnahmen 1972* (Bonn: 1973), pp. 74–75.
6. The present chairman of the Science Council. Cf. Wilhelm A. Kewenig, "Deutsche Universität von morgen," *Merkur*, Volume 31, 6, 1977.
7. Cf. Federal Conference of University Assistants, *Kreuznacher Hochschulkonzept, Reformziele der Bundesassistentenkonferenz* (Bonn: 1968); and Federal Conference of University Assistants, "Integrierte wissenschaftliche Gesamthochschule," in Klaus von Dohnanyi, ed., *Die Schule der Nation* (Düsseldorf: Econ, 1971).
8. Cf. on this point the detailed bibliography of Peter Müller, ed., *Doku-

mente zur Gesamthochschulentwicklung, Studentische Politik, special issue (Bonn-Bad Godesberg: Verlag Neue Gesellschaft, 1976).
9. Cf. Eberhard Böning, "Zum Regierungsentwurf eines Hochschulramengesetzes für die Bundesrepublik," in *Bildung und Gesellschaft,* edited by Hans Steffen (Göttingen: Vandenhoeck & Rupprecht, 1972).
10. As to the situation of comprehensive institutions in the individual Länder, cf. the compilation of Länder reports, in "Die Gesamthochschulentwicklung in den einzelnen Ländern," *Studentische Politik:* Die Gesamthochschulentwicklung zwischen Reform und Gegenreform, Volume VIII, No. 1/2 (1975).
11. Cf. the summary report "Die Gesamthochschule im Kontext der Veränderugen im tertiären Bildungswesen," *Studentische Politik, ibid.*
12. Science Council, *Empfehlungen und Stellungnahmen 1975* (Cologne: 1976), "Bericht des Vorsitzenden," p. 293.
13. *Ibid.,* p. 295.
14. Cf. Ernst v. Weizsäcker, Günther Dohmen, and Theodor Jüchter, *Baukasten gegen Systemzwänge. Der Weizsäcker-Hochschulplan* (Munich: Piper, 1970).
15. Cf. Jens Litten, *Die Sandwich-Universität oder die Hochschule für Jedermann* (Hamburg: Hoffmann & Campe, 1971).
16. Friedrich Edding, "Ansätze zum bildungspolitischen Umdenken" in Hildegard Hamm-Brücher and Friedrich Edding, *Reform der Reform —Ansätze zum bildungspolitischen Umdenken* (Cologne: Du Mont, 1973).
17. Cf. Tino Bargel and Gerhild Framhein, "Die Universität ohne Mauern," *Neue Sammlung,* Volume XV (1975), pp. 176-77.
18. For a survey of the state and the problems of the study reform see: Ludwig Huber, "Developments in Higher Education in Europe: Background Report, German Speaking Countries," Council of Europe, *Strategies for Research and Development in Higher Education,* edited by Noel Entwistle (Amsterdam: Swetz and Zeitlinger, 1976), p. 169 ff.
19. Cf. Infratest Sozialforschung, *Befragung des wissenschaftlichen Personals der Hochschulen zur Fortentwicklung von Lehre und Forschung, Wintersemester 1976/77,* Im Auftrag des Bundesministeriums für Bildung und Wissenschaft (Munich, 1977), pp. 322 ff.
20. Cf. Reinhold Merkert, "Zwischenbilanz des Fernstudiums," *Jahrbuch für Wissenschaft, Ausbildung, Schule WAS '77,* edited by Otto Peters and Heino Gollhardt (Cologne: Verlagsgesellschaft Schulfernsehen, 1977). The program "Extension Studies through Media" is to be introduced for the first time in the winter semester 1977/78 for the first year of studies in the fields of biology, electronics, mathematics, and psychology. Cf. Deutsches Institut für Fernstudien, ed., *Versuche für das Fernstudium im Medienverbund,* Zwischenbericht 1974-76. (Tübingen: 1977).
21. In contrast with the open university, the extension university of Hagen was intended to attract mostly those students who cannot personally

attend an institution because of the *numerus clausus* or for personal reasons. Cf. Johannes Rau, *Die neue Fernuniversität, Ihre Zielsetzung, ihr Aufbau und ihre geplante Arbeitsweise* (Düsseldorf: Econ, 1974), p. 78. The experience so far has been, however, that the extension university has mainly been used for adult education. In 1976, three-quarters of the "students" had already received a complete professional training. Cf. Otto Peters, "Die Fernuniversität," *Information en zur Raumentwicklung*, No. 10, 1977.
22. For project studies, cf. Egon Becker, Georg Jungbluth, Ludwig Voegelin, "Projektorientierung als Strategie der Studienreform," *Studientische Politik*, Volume V, No. 2/3 (1972).
23. Cf. "Zum Projektstudium an der Universität Bremen" in Elin-Birgit Berndt et al., *Erziehung der Erzieher: Dans Bremer Reform-Modell* (Hamburg: Rowohlt, 1972).
24. Federal-State Commission for Educational Planning and the Advancement of Research, *Information über Modellversuche im Hochschulbereich* (Bonn: 1976), p. 8.
25. Cf. *ibid.*, pp. 11–12, and pp. 53 ff.
26. Cf. Federal-State Commission for Educational Planning and the Advancement of Research, *Untersuchungen über die Verbesserung der Effizienz im Bildungswesen (Effizienzbericht)*, Appendix 2: "Verweildauer im Hochschulbereich" (Bonn: 1976), p. 3. Cf. also the partly diverging but overall supporting figures in: Federal Ministry of Education and Science, *Grund- und Strukturdaten* (Bonn: 1976), p. 100 and (1977 edition) pp. 92–93.
27. Science Council, *Empfehlungen zu Umfang und Struktur des Tertiären Bereichs* (Cologne: 1976), p. 61.
28. *Ibid.*
29. Cf. *Effizienzbericht, op. cit.*, Appendix 2, p. 18.
30. Cf. Infratest Sozialforschung, *op. cit.*, pp. 329 ff and p. 356.
31. Dietrich Goldschmidt and Sybille Funk, "Changing Concepts of the University in Society: the West German Case," in *The World Yearbook of Education 1971*, edited by Brian Holmes and David G. Scanlon (London: Evans, 1971), p. 276.

6 HIGHER EDUCATION AND THE SOCIAL CONTEXT

Manpower

When dealing with the issue of the demand for graduates, one must bear in mind the close linkage between higher education and the academic labor market. First, this means in a formal sense that graduates are oriented toward occupational positions that have traditionally been reserved for them and that ensure a high professional status. There also is a close connection with regard to the way subjects are studied in higher education. Graduates of particular disciplines as a rule move toward relatively narrowly defined professions.

In contrast, the American system of higher education allows the student to receive in a relatively short period of study, up to the first academic degree, a broad basic education which does not prejudice his subsequent choice of profession as much as the German system does. Furthermore, the student makes his choice in a labor market marked by a great degree of flexibility and transferability; only in a few occupations is a certificate of higher education the necessary prerequisite.

In the Federal Republic, the ties between the educational system and the employment system are especially strong because of the structure and hierarchy of civil service. According to legally established recruitment procedures, the criteria for placement in the civil service are the length of education and the qualifications the applicant has received during his education. There are subtle differences which allow graduates from three-year courses at teachers colleges and *Fachhochschulen* to enter only the intermediate level of civil service, while university graduates of four-year programs (in most cases, their studies have, of course, taken longer) can enter the advanced level of civil service. For the young university graduate, this means that he will be able to make a rather quick transition from the marginal social life of a student to the socially respectable, well paid position of a high-level civil servant. According to the 1970 census, 54 percent of the one million graduates from universities or teachers colleges were directly employed in the civil service; 25 percent of the graduates from *Fachhochschulen* were employed in this system. Moreover, a number of other institutions depend on public funds (e.g., many nonprofit organizations) and apply the same criteria as the civil service system. This means that almost two-thirds of all graduates from higher education are subject to the salary scales and terms of service of the civil service, while only one-third are employed in the private economy.[1] These figures clearly show that the career structure of the civil service has a guiding function for the labor market and that the linkage between the educational and the employment system at the tertiary level is very close.

This is the background against which one must discuss the question of whether the system of higher education can meet society's need for manpower. Issues concerning the economics of education raised at the beginning of the sixties in an international context, especially within the framework of the OECD,[2] had a considerable spill-over effect in that they resulted in a stock-taking of the educational and employment system of the Federal Republic of Germany. People were alarmed to realize that the number of secondary school graduates qualified for university study and graduates from institutions of higher education produced by an elitist educational system put the Federal Republic in the bottom place. Suddenly there were predictions of serious shortages in view of the rapid modernization of the expanding labor market. The first official estimate of manpower needs by the Conference of Ministers of Culture anticipated an extraordinary shortage of 300,000 teachers for the 1960s.[3]

This was the basis for Picht's sensational series of articles, "The German Educational Catastrophe." Picht argued that even a doubling of the number of qualified secondary school graduates would hardly meet the need for graduates from higher education estimated by the Conference of Ministers of Culture. He predicted deficits that would have grave consequences for the expanding German economy, especially with regard to international competition: "An educational crisis is an economic crisis. The present economic boom will soon come to an end if the younger generation, without whom no production system can function in our technological age, is not qualified."[4]

This argument for an expansion of higher education which was motivated by a predicted need for graduates, was fortified by Dahrendorf's publication "Education is a Civil Right," which caused as much of a stir. In his paper, Dahrendorf advocated an active and expansionary educational policy to abolish social inequalities in education.[5] Although based on different motivations, both arguments resulted in the same demand. They contributed significantly to a public consensus that an increasing interest in education in larger sections of the population and a significant expansion of the tertiary level were urgently needed.

This activation of educational policy, which coincided with the post-war baby boom, had surprisingly quick results. In spite of all expansionary efforts in higher education, the *numerus clausus* indicates that the system of higher education can barely cope with the on-rush of applicants and that the transition from the secondary to the tertiary level has become a bottleneck. Furthermore, since the recession that began with the oil crisis in 1973, indications of a satiation of graduates in the labor market point to a second bottleneck between the system of higher education and the employment system. The metaphor of the "dual bottleneck"[6] is a very pertinent illustration of the situation: there are more applicants for the institutions of higher education than the institutions can absorb; and there are more graduates from these institutions than the labor market for highly selective positions can absorb. This tendency is intensified because the capacity of the civil service, which in recent years has accepted two-thirds of those graduating from higher education, is decreasing, independently of the restrictions imposed by the present financial situation. In recent years, existing and newly created positions have been staffed with young graduates. This means that the average age of persons filling positions which require an academic degree has become lower and that there will be less need for replacements in the next decades.

It is especially ironic that the imminent surplus of academic graduates first became apparent in those professions which had acute deficits at the beginning of the educational campaign in the middle of the sixties and even as late as 1972. Already by 1976, because of the stagnation in public expenditures, not all graduating teachers could find a job in primary or secondary education. For 1985, the Federal-State Commission has predicted a surplus of about 136,000 to 208,000 teachers.[7] This is based on a decrease of primary and secondary students by about 40 percent as a result of: the *Pillenknick* (reduction of the birthrate due to increased use of contraception—a factor not included in earlier projections); the teacher-student ratios stipulated in the comprehensive educational plan; and the number of students that are presently studying to become teachers. Many educational politicians must feel like the magician's apprentice who cannot rid himself of the spirits he once called forth.

It must be realized, however, that even in the civil service the demand for graduates is not constant; it would be ideal, for instance, to achieve a better teacher-student ratio on the primary or secondary level, or a greater number of doctors per unit of population. The *de facto* need, however, is determined by priorities in the entire public sector. Here the dual bottleneck illustrates the dual financial burden with which the government is confronted: it must, first of all, finance the educational facilities and, secondly—as the most important employer for academic graduates—it must finance the positions in the civil service.

At present, manpower estimates are once again receiving more attention. After they had generated the first impetus for the wide-ranging educational campaign of the sixties, they were largely ignored in subsequent years when the educational euphoria had a socio-political motivation. It is not possible here to discuss in detail the complex problems of manpower projections, but the result of the four comprehensive manpower estimates worked out between 1967–1972 may be noted. They were based on the existing structures of higher education and the labor market. All of them estimated for the period until 1980 or 1985 a demand for university graduates that is below the expected number of graduates. The estimates reflect considerable variation, however, in the calculations for individual sectors. This is an indication of the methodological problems in estimating future demand.[8]

In spite of such deficiencies, a rational educational policy cannot do without manpower estimates in order to plan effectively and in the interest of the students who must decide which academic field to choose. Recently, the Federal Ministry of Education and Science ordered a number of employment projections to be made for specific fields of study. These estimates show that, except for a few disciplines such as medicine and particularly dentistry, a satiation and possibly an over-supply is expected in the labor market for university graduates for the next ten to twenty years.[9]

The expansion of education, which seems to exceed the estimated manpower requirements, has brought the question of the relation between the educational and the employment system to the forefront. As early as 1968, Hajo Riese, who a year earlier had submitted the first comprehensive estimate of graduate demand at the request of the Science Council, cautioned against an unquestioning encouragement and uncontrolled expansion of advanced education. In view of the close ties between higher education and the labor market for graduates, Riese said, such measures were only unproblematic in times of shortages. An excess supply of university graduates, however, would generate a serious imbalance between demand and supply, a situation that now seems to have developed. Riese was afraid that, in such a case, supply would have to adjust to demand, since it is a quantity that can more easily be manipulated. "The basic right to education will be of secondary importance; it is the weakest link in the chain because the economy can hardly be forced to expand its manpower."[10] Riese argued that if the objective of a basic right to education is accepted, educational research and educational policy must be oriented toward an increasing flexibility of education and professional activities.

In the meantime, the rising number of graduates has generated a strong interest in the problems of flexibility. Research on this subject is directed toward attempting to determine unexpected requirements. For example, this was investigated in the model study on the absorption of graduates from the new field of study, political science.[11] Other studies are directed toward examining the possibilities of filling vacant positions with substitute applicants who have degrees from different levels, or the possibilities of transferring university graduates from a particular academic field into different occupations. The integration of such studies into manpower estimates, however, still faces serious methodical and empirical problems.[12]

There is no doubt that at present planning in higher education is also influenced by problems in the labor market. The proposed redistribution of places at teachers colleges makes this particularly clear. A return from planning according to the demands of students to planning according to the needs of the labor market, however, is neither intended nor recommended. Such a procedure, while limiting the number of students admitted, would shift the problem of available educational facilities to another area that also has bottlenecks. There are only sporadic attempts to create educational facilities for qualified secondary school graduates outside the higher education system.[13] No matter what efforts governments and the economy will make to increase the opportunities for vocational training, they will hardly be sufficient to accommodate all those who were born during the years of a high birth-rate. Thus, to displace applicants for higher education to vocational training would only increase the problems in this sector. For this reason the president of the West German Conference of Rectors, as well as the federal government,[14] recently emphasized the fact that institutions share the responsibility of coping with the crises in the years to come. He rejected the restrictions caused by a planning procedure that would be based on the diminishing needs of the labor market for university graduates.[15]

> Our main concern must be to use the available means, which might be very limited, in such a way that as many young people as possible can receive *any meaningful education at all* after graduating from secondary school. We can only

teach this goal if the institutions of higher education also manage to admit temporarily many more students than are perhaps needed in the labor market . . . If we look at it that way, the possible excess supply of degree holders is the price to be paid for the chance of having as small a number of young people as possible who receive no education.

There is another reason why such a policy seems advisable. Up till now, university graduates have comprised a relatively small proportion of the increasing unemployment in the Federal Republic, and, according to international tendencies, it is to be expected that this will remain so even if unemployment stabilizes at a relatively high level.[16]

The discussions about flexibility, which are supposed to bring about a relaxation of the rigid linkages between higher education and employment opportunities, are a decisive factor in the attempts to alleviate the dual bottleneck: "For an active educational policy, the relations between the educational and the employment system are not constants, but variables."[17] They can be influenced if graduates become both willing and able to move and if mobility barriers —such as the recruitment policies and career structures of the employment system—are removed.

The concept of comprehensive institutions of higher education, with shorter and longer duration programs, would be an important instrument to relieve the institutions and to open up traditional career patterns. This concept, however, cannot be successful unless employment opportunities for the graduates from short-term curricula become attractive so that not all students crowd into the longer term programs because the latter are professionally more promising. In this respect it is essential that the career structure and salary scales in the civil service be revised. Already in 1971, when the OECD commission investigated the educational system of the Federal Republic, it pointed out the problems connected with such reforms. The commission considered a reform of the career system to be so difficult that:[18]

> it will make reform of education itself look like child's play. The attitudes that support it are embedded so deeply in society that only a major change in perspectives will succeed in

opening up careers to demonstrated ability and free them from their present enslavement to paper qualifications. Undoubtedly, the federal and Länder governments have a role to play here, as perhaps the worst offenders to date on this score. If they could substantially modify the present system in favor of much greater flexibility of employment for civil service jobs, they would exert a strong influence on the private sector to modify its employment practices correspondingly.

In 1974, the federal minister who had been responsible for the original governmental plan of an integrated comprehensive institution was just as pessimistic about the successful introduction of short-term studies, which would necessitate drastic changes in the systems of higher education and employment.[19]

> The perseverance of the formerly highly respected and successful German system of higher education (the Humboldt system) enables the ultra-conservatives and ultra-leftists at the universities to form their unfortunate alliance. This, and the refusal of the Federal Ministry of the Interior (which is in charge of civil servants) to concern itself seriously with these problems are unsurmountable obstacles.

This pessimistic evaluation is still valid. The timid steps to reform the career system of the civil service have not had much effect at all. Above all, such reform would need to create equal professional opportunities for graduates from three- and four-year courses of study. Yet, there are indications that the federal government intends to push this matter even against existing interest groups such as, for example, the professional associations. In 1976, the Science Council, too, had emphasized in its recommendations the need to relax the rigid structures of the employment system and to lower the expectations of university graduates with regard to their income and professional status.[20]

> Increased and broadened chances in higher education are only possible at the price of lowering the income of graduates to a certain extent while competition for top positions will rise at the same time.

The Science Council apparently intends to begin a new offensive in this critical area. Recently, a statement by the chairman of the Science Council was quoted under the heading "The Science Council has something up its sleeve." In his statement, the chairman pointed out that a student who enters a long-term course of study does so at his own risk. On the other hand, graduates from shorter courses are to have the opportunity to continue their studies later. For this reason the Chairman argued:[21]

> Higher education, whether it is short or long, should neither guarantee employment, nor should it entitle the person to a particular starting salary. If possible, all graduates should start with the same salary. A student should not decide what or how long he wants to study because of the starting salary he will receive, but because he is interested in the subject, because he is qualified, and because he believes that he can handle it.

No one knows at present whether such a rather utopian offensive to undo the links between higher education and the labor market for its graduates will be successful. Much will depend on the readiness of the unions and professional associations to represent the interests not only of their old members, but also of their potential new members by revising salary and career structures. From a sociological point of view, the possibility of rapid change in these structures which are deeply rooted in society seems remote. The quantitative aspects of labor market demands relate back to aspects of the qualitative study reform discussed in Chapter 5. As far as employment opportunities are concerned, one of the most important aspects in any revision of higher education is the need for graduates to acquire flexible skills from their education. This does not only relate to the quality of education a student receives at the university in a particular discipline; it also involves the question of general education over and above his actual academic field. Such flexible skills are particularly important in professions that require a high degree of competence because their scope of activities is not precisely defined. In this context there is some times discussion of what might be learned from the model of the liberal arts colleges in the United States.[22]

Another qualitative aspect concerns the gap between theory and practice in academic education. Representatives of the economy often criticize the fact that they have to set up costly training programs for university graduates who, after six or more years of study, enter a company but are found to be of no practical use—indeed are "over-educated" by the universities.[23] This criticism illustrates that the traditional postulate of "education through research" can produce *Fachidioten* (persons too narrowly specialized), a position that is taken both by conservative and progressive critics of the present system of higher education, albeit for different reasons. It underlines the proposition that university studies should not only include academic content, but that students should also become acquainted with the role of academia and of graduates in society and that their courses should reflect actual professional and social problems. The demand that courses should be more relevant to practical life and thus create a critical attitude on the part of the students toward their future professions has become an important part of study reform.

One quality often required in the job market for graduates concerns the graduate's social capabilities. Communication skills, psychological insight, ability to relate to other people, and leadership qualities are the most frequently expected qualities listed in newspaper advertisements for university graduates.[24] However, in the first years of their professional activity, young university graduates are keenly aware of the fact that their education did not include social or practical experiences.[25] This is an undeniable deficiency in higher education in the Federal Republic of Germany. In view of such criticism, experiments in curricular reform which include project study and practical applications or training periods are of special significance.

In summary it can be stated that, from a quantitative point of view, the system of higher education in the Federal Republic will continue to supply the graduates society needs for the foreseeable future. The problem is, rather, that the employment system must be expanded to absorb the graduates. The need for quality, however, remains. This is the challenge for curricular planning which is called upon to remedy existing deficiencies and to remain open to new developments in the labor market.

Individual Demand and Equality of Opportunity

As we discussed in the previous section, in the mid-1960s the manpower-oriented arguments for an expansion of the tertiary level of education were supplemented by those advocating an active educational policy in order to guarantee a general "civil right to education." This political demand was based on the constitutional right of every citizen to receive an education commensurate with his abilities, without consideration of his background or economic situation. The demand was meant to remove social educational barriers and to arouse an interest in education by those groups in society which until then had looked at education as something remote: "Legal equality of opportunity remains a fiction as long as people, because of their social circumstances and responsibilities, are not in a position to use their rights."[26]

Stimulated by a discussion that had already been progressing on the international level, interest in empirical studies of the extent of educational disparities between people from different social backgrounds increased. A relatively small number of educational researchers began to collect empirical data which brought into question the theory of inherent talent and thus indicated that political measures would have a definite chance of success. Originally, the burning question about existing reserves of talent had been asked in order to determine quantitative needs. Now, however, it arose again in connection with the demand for equal educational opportunities, and the answer was positive.

Educational disparities on the tertiary level relate back to the disparities on the secondary level. In the sixties, more than 90 percent of the qualified secondary school leavers actually entered a university. In the traditional three-partite secondary school system the selection mechanism already begins to work when ten or twelve-year old students enter the *Gymnasium*.

Once this decision has been made, it is hardly reversible because of the partitions between the different types of schools. It could be demonstrated that a withdrawal from secondary school prior to completion was closely related to the social circumstances of the students and his families.[27] The principal features of these circumstances were: educational and occupational level of parents, sex, religion, and regional origin.

In the mid-sixties, more than one-third of university students had parents with a university education, although less than 3 percent of the entire population had completed a university education; 5.7 percent came from working-class families, although the working class makes up 45 percent of the population.[28] Hardly one-fourth of students were women, even though they make up 50 percent of the population.[29] Some studies present a drastic picture of regional disparities—that is, the ratio between regional educational facilities and the participation of the population in education. For instance, a 1961 regional analysis of the participation of sixteen to nineteen-year olds in education showed a 12 percent participation rate in Saarland and 21 percent in Berlin. The overall average percentage by counties ranged from 3 to 48 percent, which reveals the regional disparity of educational opportunities. Finally, the analysis showed that, of 24,500 municipalities, 8,000 did not have a single sixteen to nineteen-year old person who was attending post-compulsory education on a full-time basis.[30]

The various criteria of social conditions which have a positive or negative impact on participation in education complement one another when they occur jointly. In this context the dictum became proverbial that the Catholic girl in a rural area with few educational facilities must overcome a disadvantage of 1:45 if compared with a boy of the same age in a university city in order to be able to continue her education at a *Gymnasium* or university.[31]

Toward the end of the sixties, the policy goal of equal educational opportunities and the promotion of individual demand for education had won priority over the issue of manpower requirements. The demand for education assumed special significance because it was based on the political maxim of the civil right to education (that is, it not only had a material-quantitative connotation); this was an attractive issue and brought in good publicity. For this reason, "education is a civil right" became a campaign slogan for the 1969 Bundestag elections, and consequently, in early 1970 the federal government put the educational system at the top if its reform program.

According to the general principles of educational reform that were envisaged, the educational system was to be "available to every citizen, from preschool to continuing education, for his personal, professional, and political education." This constitutional principle of equal educational opportunity was to be realized "by intensive and individual furtherance of all students on all levels of the educational system."[32]

However, it was impossible to realize these principles within the present educational system. With its outdated structures, it promoted the reproduction of existing class structures and impeded any interaction between the various educational processes. For that reason, a thorough reform of the educational system was planned. It has not been achieved yet, and individual Länder are proceeding in different ways.[33]

> In order to reach these goals, divisions between types of schools on all levels of education must disappear. By developing a differentiated system of comprehensive schools and institutions of higher education, the Federal Republic will develop a democratic and efficient system of education as it has been planned and built up in many industrial democracies in the past decades.

When this educational policy was proclaimed, the Federal Republic's educational system—policies and planning—were under analysis by the OECD. The OECD analysts considered the extent of equal opportunities one of the most important measurements of the progress of an educational system. (Hence, this was one of the central factors of the review of the German policy of education.) The analysts considered the extent of equal opportunities one of the main shortcomings which needed to be corrected, "for this is where the performance of the German educational system in the last twenty years has been most at variance with that of comparable countries."³⁴ The analysts considered the draft for a comprehensive educational plan submitted in 1971 and its long-term objectives to be principles which would measure up to the needs of a modern democratic society and would constitute a break with the educational system of the past. However, they summarized: " 'Fine words butter no parsnips' and the promises of even the smoothest rhetoric must be tested against the realities of the political-educational world."³⁵

In this context it is interesting to note that the OECD analysis, in spite of its caution of taking a too optimistic view with with regard to further economic development, still recommends the individual and not the manpower approach as the basis for educational planning in the Federal Republic. The analysts believed that manpower forecasting, the methods for which are still very inadequate, could at best be used to determine future minimum needs and not to define the desired optimum levels of education.³⁶

> Germany is a rich and prospering nation. On the whole it has underspent on educational provision in the last 20 years. We have no reason to suppose that it cannot, and should not, support a much more extended educational effort in the next 15 years. It presents, in fact, a textbook example of a country that should not seek to base its quantitative educational plans on manpower considerations. Instead, it is rich enough and economically secure enough to be asking: what kinds of citizenry do we want? What kinds of schools are likely to help us to get them? And what do we have to do to reform our present schools, qualitatively and quantitatively, in order to get the schools we need?

The orientation toward individual demand is still important in the educational policy of the Federal Republic, even if it receives varied emphasis. In 1974, that is, when the recession had already begun, the German Education Council, in its recommendations for the planning of educational research, once again stressed that "no society should refuse to recognize the wishes of as many young people as possible to continue their education. This education is part of the demand to raise the general quality of life."³⁷

The quantitative expansion of the system of higher education that has taken place since the federal government formulated its educational policy in 1970 has created the potential foundation for structural changes in favor of greater social equality. Between 1970–1976, study facilities and student numbers increased by approximately 50 percent, while the number of new entrants rose by 12 percent. To what extent did this expansion promote educational equality? In 1976, 13 percent of university students came from working-class families (1966 = 5.7 percent), and one-third of students were women (1966 = 25 percent).[38] These figures show that some progress has been achieved in involving those sectors of the population who were formerly disinterested in education or had low incomes. This statement of progress, however, needs to be modified since higher education is still characterized by a two-class system. Universities, to which the direct route is via the *Gymnasium*, have remained the preferred places of study for the higher social classes. *Fachhochschulen*, on the other hand, do not require the *Abitur* but rather a practically oriented secondary education; they have a much higher percentage of students from working-class families (28 percent).[39] The transferability that was to be facilitated by setting up comprehensive institutions of higher education was to provide a certain degree of equalization in this situation.

Financial aid for education, the regulations for which were revised in the 1971 Federal Law for the Advancement of Education (Bundesausbildungsförderungsgesetz—BAföG), is a factor that has considerably increased the prospects of individuals from low-income families to participate in post-compulsory education. Financial aid is based on the following principle: "any person who does not have the necessary means both for his living and study expenses is entitled by law to financial educational aid that will enable him to receive an education commensurate with his inclination, his aptitude, and his performance."[40]

In 1976, DM 2,470 million was spent on educational assistance for students on the secondary and tertiary level. Of this expenditure, 65 percent is carried by the Bund and 35 percent by the Länder. About 42 percent of all students in higher education were supported by two-thirds of this sum.[41] The quota of students who received financial aid through the BAföG at universities and *Fachhochschulen* gives a clear indication of the economic background of the students at various types of institutions: the quota of 63 percent at *Fachhochschulen* is far higher than the corresponding quota of 38 percent at the universities.[42] The above average provision of financial aid for disadvantaged social groups is a measure of its social policy objective: in the 1976 summer semester, for example, students from working-class families received 66 percent of the financial aid allocated while they only represented 13 percent of the total student body.[43]

In the past three years, however, there has been a slight decline in aid, with respect both to the number of students receiving assistance and to the amount granted. In 1976 an unmarried student who did not live with his parents received a maximum amount of DM 500 per month. Since the average monthly expenses of a student were around DM 640, only 30 percent of all students receiving aid could finance their studies exclusively with public aid; three years earlier 39 percent of the students had been able to do so.[44] It is hard to say at this point whether this reduction in aid is an indication of a future trend, or whether financial aid will once again rise to a higher level through continuous adjustments.

All in all, one may be somewhat skeptical over whether the trend toward equalization of opportunities on the basis of social class, sex, or region will continue in the future. The policy concept of the federal government was formulated in 1970, at a time when overall economic and political conditions were rather favorable: public interest was in favor of educational reform, and the budget for public expenditure was expected to rise. The bottlenecks in the labor market for graduates had not yet become apparent, and the educational campaign that had been initiated earlier by the Länder had aroused a great deal of interest in continuing education. In the foreseeable future, however, at least the first three of these conditions for a progressive educational plan will no longer apply. Furthermore, the decision to reach the final capacity of 850,000 study places by the beginning of the eighties, signals that the turbulent expansionary phase of the system of higher education has come to an end.

This means that it will not be possible to even out remaining regional disparities by building new universities in areas where none now exist. This is a critical point because of the fact that the attitude of students has changed considerably. Traditionally, German students tended to transfer or enroll directly in universities distant from their homes. Now, however, they are becoming increasingly immobile. Today, about 80 percent of all students would prefer to study in their native region. This means that their chances to study, as well as their choice of academic field and their choice of profession, are greatly influenced by the type of educational facilities available in their area.[45]

Regional researchers have long been critical of this attitude on the part of new students. They asked, facetiously, if the people in the area around Hanover could be expected to be especially fond of animals since the Hanover School of Veterinary Medicine had an above-average number of students from that area; or whether one could call the population around Germersheim, which has an institute for interpreters and translators, especially gifted for languages; or whether the young people of student age in South Hesse were technically more talented than those in North Hesse because more of them attend the Institute of Technology at Darmstadt.[46]

It is, of course, illusory to hope that every area of low population density can provide a fully equipped institution of higher education for qualified secondary school graduates. Also, there are many advantages to having a concentration of institutions in metropolitan rather than rural areas, while encouraging, at the same time, the mobility of students. However, from the point of view of regional policy, it seems that regionalization did not meet an optimal level when higher education was expanding.[47]

> The wave of recent establishments of new institutions of higher education in the Federal Republic of Germany—a result of the new policy move into mass higher education—has been too little related to systemwide perspectives, in spite of all the comprehensive concepts and systemwide initiatives. As a rule, concepts of higher education development are truncated on the Länder level: development di-

rections are not coordinated beyond the Länder; in the majority of cases, regional coordination of institutions comes to a dead-end at the borders of the Länder.

The following map shows the regional distribution of long-term expansion targets of higher education. It indicates those areas that have either a high or a low density of institutions of higher education, and it reveals remaining regional disparities of educational opportunity.

As far as the disparities between the social classes are concerned, structural reform of the educational system, which is supposed to facilitate transfer, was to bring about an equalization of opportunity. If students have the chance of re-entering higher education at a later time, irreversible educational decisions are avoided. Transferability between the individual types of institutions of higher education would be an important mechanism for ensuring the possibility of modifying individual study plans. This system, however, can only function if transferability operates in all directions throughout the system.

In the previous section we pointed out the problem of the linkage between academic degrees with professional opportunities. As a result of this, there is, in reality, only a one-way route from short courses to those long-term courses of study which carry the traditional rewards. Approximately 25 percent of students at *Fachhochschulen*—far more than expected—have, for example, availed themselves of the newly created possibilities of transferring into a university.

In view of the overcrowded conditions and the limited capacity of institutions of higher education, educational politicians are at present facing a dilemma. They must weigh the opportunities available to those students who are already in higher education with those of students who are waiting to be admitted. By establishing admission quotas for a second academic degree in *numerus clausus* disciplines, which are subject to the selection procedures of the ZVS, the principle of transferability has been limited in favor of students who have not yet begun their higher education. In the meantime, the admission quotas for second degrees have been fixed by the Conference of Ministers of Cul-

MAP 2
State and Long-Term Targets for the Expansion of Study Places in Higher Education, 1976–85

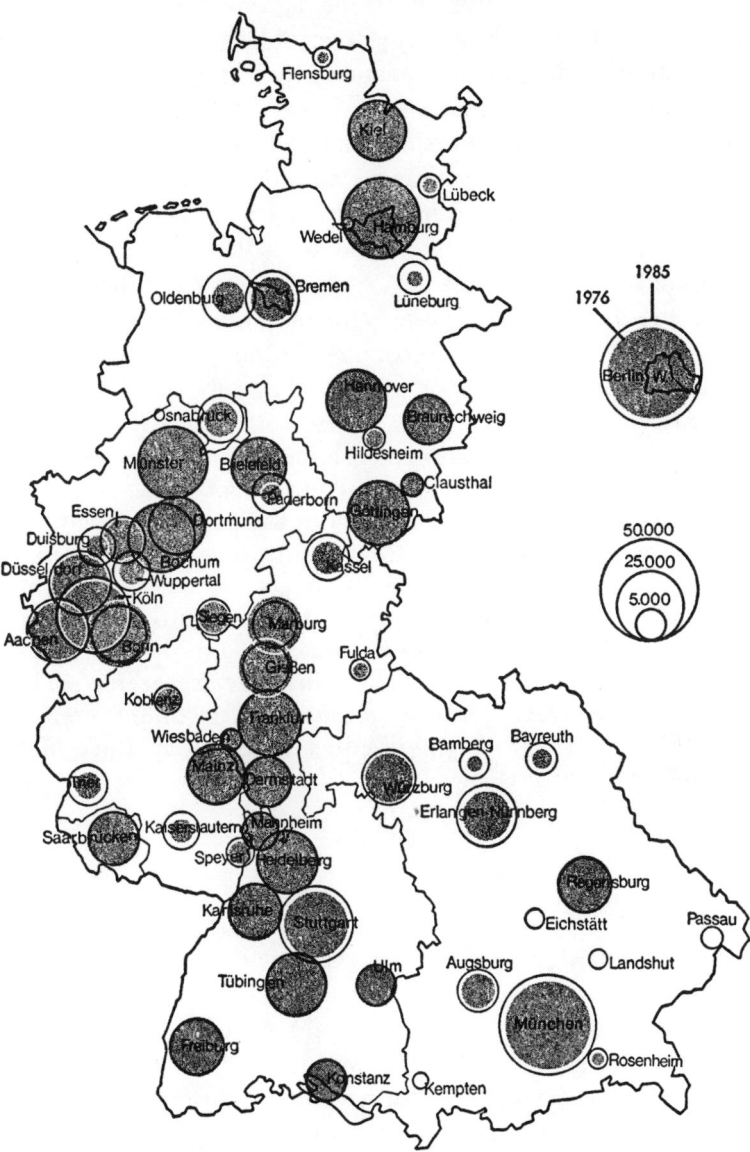

Source: Siebter Rahmenplan für den Hochschulbau, Bonn 1977, pp. 15, 22, 60-61. In several cases institutions in adjacent places are integrated into one location of higher order.

ture to be 1 percent of beginning students for medicine, and 2 percent in the other academic fields—subject to the admission procedures of the central admission agency.[48] This measure is clearly in conflict with the objective of transferability, even if its quantitative weight is moderate since it concerns only the *numerus clausus* disciplines.

The bottlenecks for admission that will continue over the next few years are also problematic in another respect. They might cause those groups who were traditionally remote from higher education to become resigned and to look, as before, for the second-best education. The result would be stagnation, perhaps even a step backward, in the movements toward greater equality of opportunity. In its 1976 recommendations, the Science Council pointed out this danger. It was feared that:[49]

> if admission to institutions of higher education becomes more difficult, especially those secondary school leavers who come from the lower social sectors of the population will be discouraged from applying to an institution of higher education. But it was in these sectors of society where the educational policy of recent years had just started to have an effect. Increased admission restrictions also indicate a discrimination between sexes in those fields that are preferred by female students. A rigorous *numerus clausus* would therefore jeopardize an essential goal of educational policy, the equality of opportunities.

Research

Humboldt conceived a close interrelation between research and teaching as the core of a university. To ensure that teaching is based on research and that students are given the chance to participate in the process of advancing knowledge, was the quality that specifically characterized university education.

Present reform concepts for higher education do not essentially diverge from this basic idea. An attempt is made to maintain the classic interrelation between research and teaching as higher education changes from education of the elite to education of the masses. In 1976, the West German Conference of Rectors stated this objectives as follows:[50]

> Research is the basis of academic teaching. Teaching at institutions of higher education must be based on the latest advances in knowledge. Only then can institutions of higher education fulfill their function of educating new generations of academics who have to safeguard the existence of our society. Only those who are active on the frontiers of knowledge themselves can judge what the latest developments of knowledge are. And only those who are directly engaged in research can be responsible for passing on knowledge to the students.

Even for *Fachhochschulen* it is demanded that they must also be given the facilities—in terms of staff and equipment—for engaging in a minimum of applied research. This is considered necessary to relate teaching to the advancement of knowledge and its practical applications.

Not everyone agrees with this position. Many believe that it is neither possible nor necessary to uphold the principle of teaching and research in its classical form when mass education on the tertiary level is introduced. Some proposals in this connection call for a direction of some teachers and students into a type of education which is just based on research knowledge and another which involves active research itself. Generally, this means a division into short and long-term programs of study, but also refers to a division of the latter into regular and graduate programs of study. Resistance to such a two-class system in higher education is prompted by historical, didactic, and social factors.

Unlike the American colleges, German universities relegated the propaedeutics for academic study from their venerable halls to the *Gymnasien* as early as the middle of the nineteenth century. In Germany, therefore, this is the place where eighteen and nineteen-year old secondary students are tested at the end of their last year for their "maturity" for university studies. Until recently, if they passed their final examination, the doors of the "alma mater" were open to them. The university was an institution which could devote itself entirely to research-based education.

The didactic principle of "learning through research" is another obstacle to the attempt to divide higher education into teaching and research-oriented academic programs. Acting in the spirit of Humboldt's thesis, reformers want to apply this classical principle not only for a privileged group, but for the entire tertiary level.[51]

Finally, behind the concept of consolidating university and non-university-type higher education into comprehensive institutions, there lies the attempt to extend the prestige of the universities to the comprehensive institutions and to minimize the differentiation by giving it a new label. The extension of the university into a comprehensive institution of higher education results in a sudden widening of the social stage, and the social ladder receives the additional support of a "nonscientific" footstool. Thus, it increases social potential, and new classes of educated citizens will be able to reap the fruits that are in such high demand. For teachers in higher education the point is especially that research enjoys a higher prestige than teaching. The difference between university professors and teachers at *Fachhochschulen* is that traditionally the former is engaged both in teaching *and* in research. Research funds permit the professor to have a cortége of assistants and other co-workers, as well as additional material resources. Last but not least, research output is the basis for the reputation and social standing of the professor. In view of these facts, it is understandable that a society divided into classes of "only teachers" and "teaching and research professors" is not very attractive. This is the background which explains the desire to extend the principle of learning through research to the entire sector of comprehensive higher education.

In reality, however, research opportunities for teachers at *Fachhochschulen* are still limited because even in comprehensive institutions the responsibilities of university teachers and of teachers at *Fachhochschulen* have not been standardized. While the teaching load of a university professor is generally eight hours per semester week, that of the professor of a *Fachhochschule* is eighteen hours per semester week. It is obvious then that the time budget of the latter is dominated by teaching functions. This corresponds with the fact that less than half of the teachers at *Fachhochschulen* state that they are engaged in research, and if so they devote to it on the average, only 14 percent of their working time.[52] A university, on the other hand, has a normative basis for research in that it expects its professors to be exponents of their academic field both in teaching and in research. The ministries of culture assume that professors spend on the average about 45 percent of their time on research. Judging from the actual experience of the professors, however, this assumed value appears to be somewhat high. They themselves state that they devote on the average no more than one-third of their time to research.[53] This self evaluation, no doubt, can only give us a rough indication since it is difficult to draw the line between the time spent on pure research and the time spent on teaching. In our following discussion of academic research, we shall limit ourselves to university-type institutions, especially to universities themselves.

Almost all university professors support the principle of a close connection between research and teaching. When a poll was taken on the research situation at the universities, 92 percent of the professors confirmed the statement that "if university professors are no longer engaged in research, their teaching becomes sterile."[54] They consider the contact with students to be a stimulating factor which also has a stimulative effect on research; yet they also complain about the growing burden of teaching and unpopular administrative duties which often make intensive research at universities impossible (74 percent).[55] Although the present research situation at universities is still considered just about adequate, almost all of the professors (90 percent) think that structural changes in the past years have brought about a deterioration of research;[56] 44 percent also believe that research in their area has already suffered considerably because of financial cut-backs in recent years.[57]

The prognosis for the future is not optimistic It is expected that the research situation in the coming years will become progressively worse.[58] If it were up to the professors questioned in this poll, however, research and teaching should remain the defining characteristics of the university professors. Two-thirds hold that research would best be served if every university professor engaged in research in addition to his teaching load; but only one-third believes that this will be the case in ten years. Rather, they expect that research will move away from the universities into pure research institutions, and also that there will be a greater differentiation between "teaching professors" and "research professors." The latter alternative is sometimes seen in connection with a differentiation of types of institutions into "normal" and "graduate" schools.[59]

This pessimistic attitude seems justified in view of enrollment increases expected over the next ten years, and in view of the fact that financial considerations will probably prohibit a continuing increase of academic staff. Indeed, there seems to be no doubt that in the forseeable future research activities will have to suffer because of the increased burden of teaching. The "temporary emergency increase" of teaching loads which will become necessary for some years in order to cope with the number of students will considerably reduce the personnel capacity available for research. Such a long-term shift of priorities from research to teaching may have serious repercussions for how the university perceives its function.

Financing University Research

It should have become clear from our previous discussion that research, and predominantly pure research, is a fundamental element of the higher education system. University research is supplemented by nonuniversity federal and state institutes with varying functions, and by research institutions outside the universities which are generally funded jointly by the Bund and the Länder. In particular these include the big science establishments (for example, the twelve centers for nuclear research, air and space travel, cancer research, mathematics and data processing, and others), the Max Planck Society (fifty-one institutes concentrating mostly on research in natural and life sciences, as well as some institutes dealing with social sciences), and the Frauenhofer Society (with twenty-nine institutes concentrating on applied technological research).

Besides these research institutes, research is also carried out by industry. Although this research is mostly financed by industry itself, about one-fifth of total expenditure is subsidized by federal ministries for specified programs.

At the beginning of the seventies, approximately 415,000 researchers were working at the institutions of higher education, at research centers outside these institutions, and in industry. Their responsibilities, however, not only included research; specifically, researchers at the universities are also engaged in teaching. When the Science Council converted the number of research workers into full-time equivalents (based on different research inputs in the various sectors), it concluded that research carried out by the various institutions was as follows:[60] universities—30 percent; research institutes outside the universities—19 percent; and research in industry—47 percent. Thus, about one-third of the research potential is located at universities.

A substantial part of the material requirements for research activities at the universities are met by funds from the state budgets. Such research funds, which are allocated through the budget and in general are progressively revised, have the big advantage of being unencumbered by administrative red tape; they do not require any special applications, interim reports, and other appraisals, which means that research can be carried out without any interruption. The disadvantage is that this system is rather rigid, and the once-determined amount is almost automatically reallocated to the same persons and institutions, and thus to the same areas of research—no matter how the problems change in importance or urgency.

However, the university budgets of the Länder are not sufficient to meet all the requirements of research. They are supplemented by other funds for which researchers may apply for specified research projects. According to a poll in the winter semester of 1976/77, almost half the academic staff at universities receive part or all of their research resources from such other sources.[61] The most important source for additional funds is the German Research Association, the central agency for the promotion of German research (52 percent of the recipients of other funds). Federal [62] and Länder departments also contribute much to research projects (26 percent and 22 percent respectively of the recipients), as well as private enterprises (22 percent). Other contributors are the foundations (which provide funds to 11 percent of recipients). In spite of the low percentage of their share, the function of the foundations is an important one because the rules governing the use of their research grants are less bureaucratic and more flexible.

German Research Association

These percentages do not reveal the amounts of money the universities receive. Exact figures can only be given for the most important agency, the German Research Association (Deutsche Forschungsgemeinschaft—DFG). The amount of research funding granted by the DFG in 1976 was around DM 581 million.[63] The distribution according to research areas can be shown for DM 545 million. Of this amount, 36 percent went to life sciences (biology, medicine, agricultural sciences), natural sciences received

TABLE 15
Research Promotion by the DFG according to Academic Field, 1976
(in percent)

Medicine, Nutritional Research	20.4
General Engineering Sciences and Mechanical Engineering	14.2
Biology	10.9
Physics	8.7
Geological Sciences (Oceanography, etc.)	7.9
Chemistry	7.0
History and Art	5.6
Social Sciences	5.4
Architecture, Urban Construction, Civil Engineering	5.2
Electronics	3.0
Agricultural and Forestry Sciences	2.9
Languages and Literatures	2.7
Theology, Philosophy, Psychology, Pedagogics	2.2
Veterinary Medicine	1.9
Mining and Metallurgical Engineering	1.2
Mathematics	0.8
Total	100.0

24 percent, engineering sciences 24 percent, and humanities and social sciences 16 percent. Breaking this down further to the level of specific fields the priorities in expenditure appear in Table 15.[64] The funding policy of the German Research Association mainly consists of three procedures. Normal Procedure Grants (*Normalverfahren*) which comprise approximately one-third of its fund; Priority Procedure Grants (*Schwerpunktverfahren*), which amount to one-fifth; and Special Research Areas (*Sonderforschungsbereiche*), which total one-third. The research funds of the DFG come almost entirely from the Bund and the Länder (57 percent and 42 percent respectively).[65] The Bund contributes 70 percent to the funding of special research areas, a figure that from 1978 on will be raised to 75 percent. Financing of the other procedures is divided 50:50 between the Bund and the Länder.

The Normal Procedure Grant (1976 = DM 197 million) is the traditional DFG grant. The initiative for this grant comes from the applying researchers, and no central planning or specific focus is involved. These funds are sometimes characterized as providing the "topsoil" of the German research landscape.

In spite of its earlier aversion to planning, the DFG has for several years increasingly taken the opportunity to supplement research resources systematically, to define research goals, and above all to initiate research in new areas. In its annual report for 1969 the DFG stated that "research planning, a concept that had been banned from the vocabulary of the DFG for an entire epoch, has become an obligation."[66]

With its Priority Procedure Grants initiated in 1950 (1976: 110 programs with a total of DM 112 million), the DFG has in fact practiced outright research planning for a considerable time. This procedure is based on the priorities established by university representatives in DFG committees which apply scientific and politico-scientific criteria to define those areas of research that have either been neglected or require specific attention. The DFG budget then provides the basis for the funding of such areas, and the universities are urged through colloquia, discussions with experts, and publications to focus their attention on such research.

On the suggestion of the Science Council, the first Special

Research Areas were established in 1968. In 1976 there were 114 such special research areas and the amounts allocated to them had grown to DM 205 million. These allocations involve detailed planning in which universities, the Länder, the Bund and the Science Council participate in DFG committees. Each special research area is concentrated at one particular university, so that these long-term projects are pursued at institutions that are specifically well-equipped for the subject in terms of personnel and facilities. This is a conscious attempt to establish different research foci at different universities, a division of labor that was considered abhorent at a time when research subjects were not as varied and required less funds. In the preliminary evaluation of proposed research areas by referees appointed by the DFG priority is given to the following questions:[67] Is the research subject of the special research area to be supported for scientific reasons? Is the research subject to be supported for politico-scientific reasons? Is the research project to be supported for social reasons?

Research promotion by the DFG is based on the evaluation of research applications that follows different procedures according to the three types of allocation. The evaluations involve the honorary collaboration of several hundred academics in the specific disciplinary and the central-planning and decision-making committees. The fact that members of all universities cooperate in DFG committees clearly illustrates the position of this central institution as an integral component of the decentralized system of higher education.

The outcome of DFG planning procedures since 1961 is published in the so-called "grey plans"; the fifth plan of 1976 is current at the present time.[68] In order to prepare this last plan, 1,350 academics were asked for their expert opinion; 70 percent responded. In addition, suggestions were made by other scientific organizations, as well as the Bund and the Länder. Within one and a half years, 120 representatives of the universities worked out the basic outlines for the plan through individual contributions and several committee meetings. After the Science Council adds its comments to these plans, they become the basis for the intermediate-term financial planning of the Bund and the Länder.

These intermediate-term plans, as well as the entire evaluation and decision-making of the DFG, are a great burden on the academics, especially on the most capable of them. There are frequent complaints, but so far no alternative has been found that would not also reduce the advantages of this procedure.

Foundations

The foundations, which have pinpointed their own research policy, play an important part as far as the availability of additional research funds is concerned. Following is a table listing the most important foundations and their research contributions:[69]

TABLE 16
Major Foundations Contributions to Research

Foundation	Origin of Funds Foundation Assets	Contribution to Research Year	DM Million
Volkswagen Foundation	1,400 million	until 1971 annually	
			135.0
		1975	62.0
Federation of Donors for German Science	Annual contributions from industry	1975	39.2
Robert Bosch Foundation	259 million	1972	17.5
Fritz Thyssen Foundation	105 million	1961–71 approx. annually	12.0
Alfried Krupp von Bohlen und Halbach Foundation	500 million	1972	4.0
Mahle Foundation	61 million	1972	3.8
Werner Reimers Foundation	60 million	until 1972 annually	3.0

The allocation of foundations is dependent on the overall economic condition of the country. This is the reason, for example, why the Volkswagen Foundation had to reduce its research grants by 78 percent from 1964 to 1973—from DM 212 million to DM 47 million. By comparison, the DFG is a relatively reliable organization even though the recession has left its mark in recent years on the DFG's capacity to promote research.

The foundations pay special attention to lacunae in German research, whether these relate to shortcomings in basic research or current social problems. In the early 1960s, for instance, the Thyssen Foundation responded to the problem of intellectual reserves by funding several years of empirical studies on "talent and educational reserves." As far as higher education is concerned, the Volkswagen Foundation financed, among other projects, the "working group for empirical educational research" at the University of Heidelberg; it also supplied the initial funds for the "German Institute for Extension Studies" (Deutsches Institut für Fernstudien—DIFF) and the "Institute for the Teaching of Natural Sciences" (Institute für die Pädagogik der Naturwissenschaften—IPN). Most important perhaps, the Volkswagen Foundation founded the "Information System for Higher Education" (Hochschul-Informations-System—HIS) and supplied the funds for it until it was included in the government budget.

As a rule, the foundations impose a time limit on the foci of the research they support; these are adjusted as research needs change. The Volkswagen Foundation uses the following criteria in its funding policy:[70] originality and quality; interdisciplinary cooperation; international comparison of subject matters; opportunity for productive international cooperation; possible contributions to the definition and solution of socially important issues; and new fields of investigation, combined with a reform of research and teaching.

As far as possible, the foundations only finance the establishment and early years of new research activities that may turn out to be long-term projects. If such projects appear promising, they are expected to be taken over by government agencies, so that opportunities for the foundations to initiate new activities are not unduly limited over the course of time.

Social Relevance

Looking at the impact of university research on issues of social relevance, the past two decades have shown a significant change.

The possible contribution of university research to the solution of current social problems has become an important criterion for research planning. It is of growing significance in social sciences and generally in the selection and support of research projects that are of special interest. This has already led some people to warn against placing too much emphasis on this criterion and particularly its indiscriminate application (e.g., with regard to the humanities where such aspects can be taken into consideration less frequently). Also it must be noted that the increasing research activity funded by state departments mainly proceeds from such premises. This means that university research has the important function of assuring a sufficiently broad range of basic research to counterbalance such a tendency. Basic research may not appear to be relevant to current social problems at first glance, but it creates the conditions which allow other types of research to be carried out.

University professors themselves are more and more leaving their academic ivory towers. Contrary to former times, a greater number of scientists today are either temporarily or permanently involved in the public sector. The advisory function of scientists in political matters has become quite important because of the government's growing involvement in research and planning. The methodical and politico-scientific questions that have resulted from this have led to the development of a separate, flourishing branch of science.

FOOTNOTES

1. According to an estimate by the Ministry of Culture of Baden-Württemberg in its report on the situation in the area of higher education, "Situation im Hochschulbereich." Cf. Parliament of Baden-Württemberg, Printed Matter 6/7226 of March 3, 1975, p. 17.
2. Cf. OECD, *Policy Conference on Economic Growth and Investment in Education* (Paris: 1962).
3. Cf. Conference of Ministers of Culture, *Bedarfsfeststellung 1961 bis 1970* (Stuttgart: Klett, 1963).

4. Georg Picht, *Die deutsche Bildungskatastrophe* (Olten und Freiburg: Walter, 1964). This book was originally published as a series of articles under the same heading in the weekly *Christ und Welt*.
5. Cf. Ralf Dahrendorf, *Bildung ist Bürgerrecht* (Hamburg: Nannen, 1965).
6. This is the title of a collection of articles on the problems of German higher education. Cf. Ulrich Lohmar and Gerhard E. Ortner, eds., in collaboration with Manfred Bayer, *Der doppelte Flaschenhals—Die deutsche Hochschule zwischen Numerus clausus und Akademikerarbeitslosigkeit* (Hannover: Schroedel, 1975).
7. Cf. Federal-State Commission for Educational Planning, *Ergebnisse der bisherigen Untersuchungen zur Prognose des Lehrerangebots und Lehrerbedarfs* (Stand 24, July 1974), Dokumentation K 25/74.
8. These are the following estimates of requirements: Hajo Riese, *Die Entwicklung des Bedarfs an Hochschulabsolventen in der Bundesrepublik Deutschland* (Wiesbaden: Steiner, 1967); A. Krafft, H. Sanders, and P. Straumann, under the direction of Hans Peter Widmaier, *Hochqualifizierte Arbeitskräfte in der Bundesrepublik Deutschland bis 1980*, Federal Ministry of Education and Science, Series Hochschule 6 (Bonn: 1971); Laszlo Alex and Heinrich Heuser, *Angebot und Bedarf an hochqualifizierten Arbeitskräften in der Bundesrepublik Deutschland bis 1980*, Federal Ministry of Education and Science, Series Hochschule 8 (Bonn: 1972); German Institute for Economic Research, *Projektion der Qualifikationsstruktur des Arbeitskräftebedarfs in den Wirtschaftsbereichen der BRD bis 1985* (Berlin: 1972). For a good survey of the results cf. Parliament of Baden-Württemberg, *op. cit.* (Footnote 1).
9. Projections that apply to specific academic areas were made upon the request of the Federal Ministry of Education and Science for the following disciplines so far: engineers and natural scientists; economists; law and social scientists; and students of medicine. For a survey of these as well as of other prognoses cf. "Die Zukunft der Hochschulabsolventen—Eine Übersicht über 23 Akademikerprognosen der 'zweiten Generation,'" *Materialien aus der Arbeitsmarkt- und Berufsforschung*, July 1976.
10. Hajo Riese, "Theorie der Bildungsplanung und Struktur des Bildungswesens," *Konjunkturpolitik*, Volume XIV, numbers 5–6 (1968), p. 226.
11. Cf. Dirk Hartung, Reinhard Nuthmann, and W. D. Winterhager, *Politologen im Beruf*, Zur Aufnahme und Durchsetzung neuer Qualifikationen im Beschäftigungssystem (Stuttgart: Klett, 1970).
12. For a survey of the educational-economic developments in the Federal Republic of Germany cf. Laszlo Alex, "Absolventenangebot und berufliche Flexibilität (Strategie der Bildungsökonomie: von der punktuellen Bedarfsrechnung zum integrierten Prognosesystem der 'dritten Generation')," in *Der doppelte Flaschenhals*, *op. cit.* (footnote 6) Cf. also Ulrich Teichler, Dirk Hartung, and Reinhard Nuthmann, *Hoch-*

schulexpansion und Bedarf der Gesellschaft (Stuttgart: Klett, 1976), especially Chapter 3.
13. Cf. German Educational Council, *Abitur—und kein Studium*, Gutachten und Studien der Bildungskommission, Vol. 32 (Stuttgart: Klett, 1974).
14. Cf. for example the statement to the press by the undersecretary of the Federal Ministry of Education and Science, Professor Jochimsen, "Verstärkte Bemühungen um Abstimmung von Bildungs- und Beschäftigungssystem," Federal Ministry of Education and Science, *Informationen* (May 1976), pp. 91 ff.
15. West German Conference of Rectors, *Qualität und Quantität—Die Hochschulen im Schatten des Studentenberges*, Dokumente zur Hochschulreform XXX/1977 (Bonn-Bad Godesberg, 1977), pp. 22–23.
16. Cf. Manfred Tessaring and Heinz Werner. *Beschäftigungsprobleme von Hochschulabsolventen im internationalen Vergleich*, Kommission für wirtschaftlichen und sozialen Wandel, Volume 53 (Göttingen: Schwartz, 1975), pp. 405 ff.
17. Laszlo Alex, "Absolventenangebot und berufliche Flexibilität, *op. cit.*, (footnote 12), p. 100.
18. OECD, *Reviews of National Policies for Education: Germany* (Paris: OECD, 1972), p. 106.
19. Hans Leussink, "Fünf Jahre bundesweite Bildungsplanung," *Bildungspolitik mit Ziel und Mass*, Festschrift for Wilhelm Hahn (Stuttgart: Klett, 1974), p. 91.
20. Science Council, *Empfehlungen zu Umfang und Struktur des Tertiären Bereichs* (Cologne: 1976), p. 57.
21. Cf. the article "Der Wissenschaftsrat führt etwas im Schilde: Revolution von oben her an den Universitäten," *Stuttgarter Zeitung* (August 31, 1977).
22. Cf. Science Council, *op. cit.* (footnote 20), p. 68.
23. Cf. for example, West German Conference of Rectors, Die Hochschulen und ihre Leistung in der Gesellschaft (Jahresversammlung 1972), *Dokumente zur Hochschulreform XIX/1972* (Bonn-Bad Godesberg: 1972), pp. 84–85.
24. Cf. Tino Bargel and Gerhild Framhein, "Zur Diskussion von Bildungszielen und zur Leistungsmessung im Hochschulbereich," in *Soziale Indikatoren III*, edited by Wolfgang Zapf (Frankfurt/M: Campus, 1976).
25. Cf. Gerhild Framhein, Hansgert Peisert, "Graduates' Views on Higher Education." In A. Bonboir, ed., *Instructional Design in Higher Education—Innovations in Curricula and Teaching*. Proceedings of the 2nd Congress of the European Association for Research and Development in Higher Education. (Louvain-la-Neuve: 1976), pp. 300–1.
26. Ralf Dahrendorf, *op. cit.*, p. 9.
27. Cf. Hansgert Peisert and Ralf Dahrendorf, eds., *Der Vorzeitige Abgang vom Gymnasium*, (Bildung in neuer Sicht, Series A, No. 6) (Villingen: Neckar-Verlag, 1967).

28. Cf. Federal Ministry of Education and Science, *Bildungsbericht '70* (Bonn: 1970), p. 97.
29. Cf. Gerhard Kath et al., *Das soziale Bild der Studenten in der Bundesrepublik Deutschland*, Deutscher Bundestag, Printed Matter 7/2803 (Bonn: 1974), p. 38.
30. Cf. Hansgert Peisert, *Soziale Lage und Bildungschancen in Deutschland* (Munich: Piper, 1967), pp. 24 ff., 29 ff., and 51 ff.
31. Cf. *ibid.*, pp. 19 ff.
32. *Bildungsbericht '70, op. cit.*, p. 9.
33. *Ibid.*, p. 9.
34. OECD, *op. cit.*, p. 55.
35. *Ibid.*, p. 70.
36. *Ibid.*, p. 107.
37. German Educational Council, *Aspekte für die Planung der Bildungsforschung*, Empfehlungen der Bildungskommission (Bonn: 1974), p. 61.
38. Results of a representative poll at universities, Fachhochschulen and teacher colleges. Cf. Deutsches Studentenwerk, Vorauswertung der 8. Sozialerhebung Sommersemester 1976 (Bonn: 1976), pp. 4–5.
39. Cf. *ibid.*, p. 17.
40. Federal Law for the Individual Support of Education (Bundesausbildungsförderungsgesetz —BAföG), Article 1.
41. Cf. Federal Ministry of Education and Science, *Jahresbericht 1976* (Bonn: 1977), p. 16.
42. Cf. Deutsches Studentenwerk, *op. cit.*, p. 17.
43. Cf. *ibid.*, p. 6.
44. Cf. *ibid.*, pp. 6–7.
45. Cf. the basic analysis by Clemens Geissler, *Hochschulstandorte—Hochschulbesuch*, Regionale Herkunst und Bildungswanderung der deutschen Studierenden (Hannover: 1967); also Heiner Monheim, "Die raumordnungspolitische Relevans des Hochschulbaus,"*Informationen zur Raumentwicklung*, No. 3/4 (1977), p. 207.
46. Robert Geipel, *Bildungsplanung und Raumordnung* (Frankfurt/M.: Diesterweg, 1968), p. 37.
47. Robert Geipel, "Hochschulgründungen und Regionalpolitik," in *Der doppelte Flaschenhals, op. cit.*, (Footnote 6), p. 185.
48. Cf. Central Agency for Student Admissions, *Zweiter Bericht mit Materialien zu den Vergabeverfahren 1974–76*. Dortmund, p. 15.
49. Science Council, *op. cit.*, (Footnote 20), pp. 42–43.
50. West German Conference of Rectors, *Arbeitsbericht 1976* (Bonn-Bad Godesberg, 1977), Appendix 31: "Zur Sicherung der Forschung in den deutschen Hochschulen," p. 205.
51. Cf. Federal Conference of University Assistants, *Forschendes Lernen—Wissenschaftliches Prüfen* (Bonn: 1970), p. 7.
52. Cf. Infratest Sozialforschung, *Befragung des wissenschaftlichen Personals der Hochschulen zur Fortentwicklung von Lehre und Forschung*, Win-

tersemester 1976/77, Im Auftrag des Bundesministeriums für Bildung und Wissenschaft (Munich: 1977), pp. 253 ff. (and in the volume of tables, part 3, table 2.3).
53. Cf. *ibid.*, pp. 262 ff.
54. Cf. Institut für Demoskopie Allensbach, *Die Lage der Forschung an den deutschen Universitäten*, Erster Bericht über eine Repräsentativbefragung, *Auf Anregung der Deutschen Forschungsgemeinschaft* (Allensbach: 1977), p. 7.
55. Cf. *ibid.*, p. 7.
56. Cf. *ibid.*, p. 11.
57. Cf. *ibid.*, p. 8.
58. Cf. *ibid.*, p. 11.
59. Cf. *ibid.*, p. 10.
60. Cf. Science Council, *Empfehlungen zur Organisation, Planung und Förderung der Forschung* (Bonn: 1975), pp. 14 ff.
61. Cf. for this and the following statements Infratest Sozialforschung, *op. cit.*, p. 287.
62. For more information about the financing of projects and focal points of research of the federal departments cf. Federal Ministry of Research and Technology, *Bundesbericht Forschung V* (Bonn: 1975).
63. Cf. German Research Association, *Tätigkeitsbericht 1976*, Volume 1 (Bonn-Bad Godesberg: 1977), p. 17.
64. Cf. *ibid.*, pp. 32 ff.
65. Cf. *ibid.*, p. 238.
66. Quotation from Thomas Nipperdey and Ludwig Schmugge, *50 Jahre Forschungsförderung in Deutschland*, Ein Abriss der Geschichte der Deutschen Forschungsgemeinschaft 1920–1970 (Bonn: 1970), p. 104.
67. Cf. German Research Association, *Mitteilungen 4/1974* (Bonn-Bad Godesberg: 1974), p. 45.
68. Cf. German Research Association, *Aufgaben und Finanzierung V, 1976–78* (Boppard: Harald Boldt Verlag, 1976).
69. Cf. Science Council (Footnote 60), *op. cit.*, pp. 74 ff.
70. Cf. Volkswagen Foundation, *Bericht 1975/76* (Hannover: 1976), p. 10.

7 EFFICIENCY

To conclude this study, we would like to comment on the efficiency of planning, administration, and coordination of the system of higher education. In this respect it must be remembered that the German system of higher education is currently not in a phase of continuous reform, but rather is in a phase of reconstruction that involves making essential changes. This refers to both content and form of higher education, as well as to management structures. It is therefore sometimes difficult to differentiate between short-term obstacles and long-term structural problems. A case in point is the stir caused by the "capacity regulations" and their amendments.

In this chapter, we will focus our attention on three key problems of special significance for the efficiency of the system of higher education: the structure of planning bodies; cooperation between the Bund and the Länder; and relations between government and institutions of higher education. In discussing these three issues, we will draw on the comments of leading representatives of the higher education sector itself.

Planning Bodies

With Prussian thoroughness, the Federal Republic has in recent years developed a planning system that has already had considerable impact through the comprehensive educational plan and the frame plans for construction in higher education. Simultaneously, a plethora of planning and coordinating agencies has been established. They have a latent potential for growth that might well lead to Parkinsonian dimensions.

Let us take a look at the tip of this iceberg of planning and coordinating committees staffed either by government officials or by a mixture of members: the Federal-State Commission for Educational Planning (Bund-Länder-Kommission für Bildungsplanung—BLK) and its committee for research promotion; the Planning Committee for Construction in Higher Education, the Science Council, the Conference of Ministers of Culture (Kultusministerkonferenz—KMK). All of these have numerous subcommittees and working groups, and—except for the Planning Committee—their own central office. In each of these five agencies, the Länder are represented by ministers, except for Bavaria and Lower Saxony who have delegated "only" an undersecretary to the administrative commission of the Science Council. The fifty-five seats in these committees to be filled by the Länder are held by eighteen government officials. Since seven of these officials have only one seat each, the remaining eleven ministers hold forty-eight seats, more than four per person. The Bund which participates in four agencies (not in the KMK which is purely a Länder agency) is represented by the ministers of education and finance, as well as by undersecretaries from other ministries. The twenty-two seats in the four agencies to be held by the Bund are filled by eleven persons. This accumulation of functions is shown in Diagram F, in which the positions held in personal union are emphasized.

As a rule, the ministers in these agencies are advised and accompanied by their undersecretaries who are at the same time members of the subcommittees and working groups. Furthermore, they represent their ministry in other agencies, for example, in the central agency for student admission (Zentralstelle für die Vergabe von Studienplätzen—ZVS) which in turn has numerous committees, or in the administrative commission for extension studies in association with the media. If one takes into consideration that these agencies meet rather frequently,[1] the "overload quota" on high officials from the ministries of culture of the Bund and the Länder is impressive. It is, however, also alarming to think of the way in which these peripatetic ministers and their co-workers must attend to their difficult responsibilities. An especially critical member stated that this was one of the reasons why the educational reform is so slow in coming:[2]

> The worst is that most of those responsible (I don't except myself) are hardly aware of their collective inability to carry

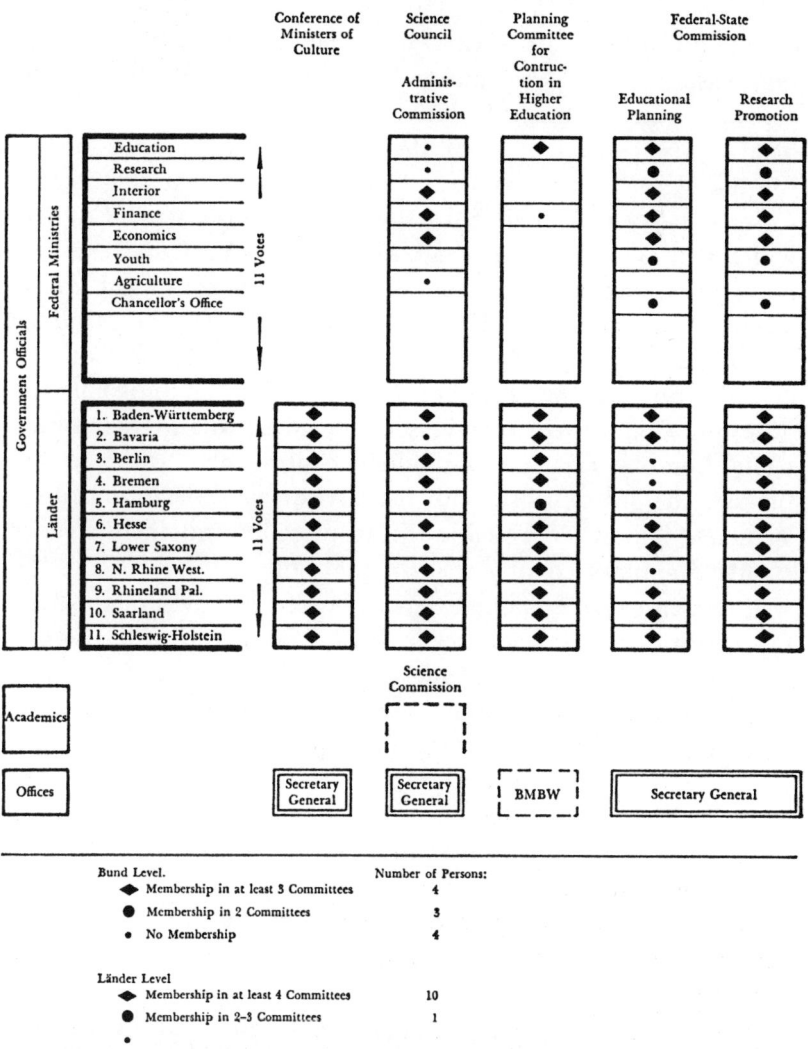

DIAGRAM F
Accumulated Membership in Top Agencies Composed of Federal and Länder Members

out reforms because they are worn out by the battle with details. Because of the prodigious activities that only appear to be efficient, and because of the glut of necessary information, these people have not time for reforms if they want to survive in office. They can seldom or not at all afford the necessary distance or time for reflection that is needed to get an overall picture of the situation.

As early as 1971, K. H. Hasemann, one of the most experienced cultural officials of this circle, had asked whether this system was efficient. Hasemann was the secretary general of the Science Council from 1966–1971, and from 1970 on he was the head of the central office of the Federal-State Commission. In the so-called "Hasemann Paper"[3] he suggested that the Science Council be consolidated with the German Education Council, which still existed at that time. He also suggested that the Federal-State Commission be combined with the planning committee for Construction in Higher Education. That is, he suggested that advisory (Science Council and German Education Council) and decision-making agencies (Federal-State Commission and Planning Committee) remain separate to maintain their objectivity, but that each use a common central office which would prepare the groundwork both the advisory and decision-making agencies.[4] This would enable the agencies to avail themselves of standardized and equally efficient preliminary material.

Hasemann recommended that the representatives of the Länder continue to use their own administrations in order to prepare their decisions independently. In this way, pending problems and plans would simultaneously be transferred to the executive branch of the government in question—a necessary prerequisite to carry out decisions in the way intended by the agencies. Indeed Haseman also realistically pointed out that an amalgamation of the two planning and decision-making agencies (BLK and Planning Committee) would require another amendment to the Constitution. No one could count on that, however, unless "the present system clearly has proved to be a failure or too unwieldy."[5]

The profusion of policies and plans generated by the top agencies has a multiplying effect on directives to the lower levels of cultural offices of the Länder. It constantly elicits the reaction of the central coordinating committees and of the universities themselves. This has led to a considerable increase of work which is reflected in numerous commentaries, appraisals, plans, ordinances, and laws. They illustrate the range of viewpoints and the creative chaos of a pluralistic, decentralized system, but make it difficult for anyone to be aware of how things stand. Indeed, it may now be even more evident how unwieldy this complicated system is, but no measures have been taken to make it more efficient.

Earlier, we called attention to the work overload of the high-level cultural officials. However, mention must also be made of the academics who cooperate on an honorary basis in these systemwide advisory and coordinating commissions. It is true that fewer of them are members in multiple committees than are the cultural officials, but they do not have their own staff of co-workers. In general, their functions must be pursued side by side with their regular duties as university professors. This means that they often experience a conflict of duties which may jeopardize their ability to fulfill the special tasks that are so important for educational policy with the necessary concentration and promptness expected of select experts. Individual suggestions that experts be temporarily appointed to full-time advisory positions have so far not been heeded. In consequence, this means that permanent employees in the central offices have an important influence on the elaboration of recommendations and decisions of the experts, a fact which has—fortunately—closed many a gap in the catalogue of tasks.

The inflated number of agencies and of meetings on the systemwide level is matched by the number of meetings and administrative waste in the individual institutions of higher education. Planning and decision-making tasks have multiplied because of the transformation of many institutions into large-scale enterprises which are hard put to rid themselves of archaic inefficient administrative structures. This coincides with the necessary process to make institutions of higher education more democratic, a process that has led to broad cooperation of the various groups of university members in the decisions on all levels.

Planning departments have meanwhile been created at all larger universities. Their counterparts are committed but dilettante university members of all groups who participate in the various planning activities through the committees on all levels of the university—from the lower level of departmental committees to various commissions and the central committees which decide on development planning, budgetary estimates, determination of student admissions, questions of research planning, and so forth.

The problems of planning procedures at the university level have become especially apparent now that the institutional development plans are being set up. The necessary coordination of divergent interests within and among the various committees has brought about laborious and sometimes nerve-racking procedures. Planning activities have been hampered by the absence of detailed criteria and guidelines on the part of the ministries of culture. As a consequence, the individual development plans for institutions of higher education are only partly compatible on the Länd level, not to mention the Bund level. Standardization of development planning will be an important task in the years to come.

The fact that university members take part in the internal decision-making processes will have its effect on the time they have available for and the efficiency of their academic work. The price they have to pay for their participatory rights is an inflation of meetings and committee work which often render the decision-making process ponderous and inefficient.

The president of the West German Conference of Rectors said in this connection:[6]

> The reorganization that took place in recent years under the cloak of university reforms has presented us with a self-administrative structure whose inherent unwieldiness will prevent it from measuring up to the tasks of the coming years. Although we do not question the principle of a group university—this would only create obstructions we cannot afford—we need technical experts to do the spadework and to tighten the system with a firm hand. In general, those in charge must be prepared to delegate responsibilities.

The executive organs will have to have more authority, especially if faculty committees are unable to reach decisions that are subject to deadlines.

From a technical point of view, such measures would indeed seem necessary in order to break the vicious cycle that is bound to occur if the diversity of decision-making increases further, while universities insist on maintaining or even broadening the scope of self-administration. Moreover, problems will become more complex and will require increasing preparation on the part of committee members; this may easily lead to a further increase in academic meetings and to problems of communication between the few professional planners and the many autodidacts.

Due to the nature of the university as an institution, and because of the rights to self-administration which the other university groups have just attained after a long struggle against the traditional university organization, it is doubtful that technical administrative efficiency will receive greater attention in the future development of universities.

Cooperation Between Bund and Länder

Based on the cultural autonomy of the Länder, the decentralized system of higher education in the Federal Republic has—as we have shown—increasingly been supplemented by elements of central coordination, planning, and decision making. The present form, a mixture of central and decentralized elements, can prove to be efficient if the idea of a cooperative cultural federalism is realized both horizontally and vertically. It will be inefficient if cooperation between divergent interests can only be brought about through coercion. This would restrict creativity and decision making to such a degree that neither the central nor the decentralized elements could be used to their full advantage, and the mixed system would be at a stalemate. The present mixed system frequently makes it difficult to find out where the responsibilty for decisions regarding higher educational policy rests. If wrong decisions have been made, no one wants to take the blame, while everyone claims to have a share in successful decisions.

Hence, a key problem for the efficiency of our system of higher education is the quality of cooperation between the Bund and the Länder. In review of our study we should like to come back to this question once again.

The main reason behind the trend toward centralization was the desire to obtain better systemwide planning. The difficulty of producing efficient central planning in a decentralized system led almost inevitably to the establishment of supplementary nationwide bodies and procedures. Since this restricted the authority of the Länder, they approved of the new central planning and decision-making agencies only reluctantly, acting out of necessity rather than out of conviction. The mixed Bund-Länder system practiced since 1970 represents a compromise which is not altogether adequate.

The Länder charge that the Bund—particularly in the area of construction in higher education—is using the instrument of the common tasks to impose rigid and bureaucratic controls in order to gain influence on the Länder and, through them, on higher education. The Bund, on the other hand, is unsatisfied with its limited possibilities of influencing decisions. It is true that the Bund can submit its proposals and ideas as an equal partner; however the effectiveness of the Bund still depends on the ability of the Länder to reach consensus in their decision making (horizontal cooperation).

The Länder counter the criticism that they cannot reach joint decisions by pointing to agreements that they have made without the Bund. A prominent example which is often quoted is the prompt procedure for concluding the first state contract (without the Bund!) for the placement of students. This example, however, is not very convincing considering that this agreement was largely decreed in substance and timing by the verdict of the Federal Constitutional Court. The involvement of the Bund in the planning and decision-making responsibilities of the ministerial round table of the Länder has had a similar effect as the verdict of the Federal Constitutional Court in that it promotes to some extent a solidarization of the Länder vis-à-vis the interest of the Bund.

However, apart from such formal aspects of increased solidarity, the political consensus of the Länder has declined since the middle of the sixties when cultural ministers became more partisan, in accordance with the increased political polarization of those Länder that had CDU/CSU governments and those that had SPD/FDP governments. In the course of time, this has also resulted in increased weight of proportional arguments with regard to the representation of "A"-countries (SPD/FDP) and "B"-countries in the multitude of systemwide committees; this resembles the consideration of proportional representation of religious denominations in earlier times.

Looking back to the first years of cooperation after the "common tasks" had become constitutional, the former undersecretary in the Federal Ministry of Education and Science very clearly expressed her frustration over the limited ability of the Länder to reach a consensus. She considered the dilemma of educational policy to be caused by the fact that:[7]

> Whatever good intentions there are to introduce educational reforms, they fail because constitutionally, organizationally, and institutionally the Länder are unable to implement the reforms. On the other hand, the will to reform is weakened by this inability; the result is that those who want to reform are driven into resignation (or into becoming radicals!).

The undersecretary believes that insufficient cooperation between the Länder is the source of this dilemma:[8]

— Each Land decides on the basis of the political constellation of its own government and with an eye on the next election.
— Each Land decides if, and which, reforms and expansionary steps are to be taken on the secondary and tertiary level of education; it decides on the extent, the means, and the time for such measures;
— Each Land decides the amount of educational expendi-

ture; it decides on the focal points for reforms or on no reforms, on educational curricula, objectives, the organization of schools, the kind and extent of teacher education.

Naturally, this also provides the individual Länder with an opportunity to carry out reforms on their own, which can be an asset in developing the educational system. But such procedures are inefficient for nationwide planning. The former undersecretary viewed the procedures of the Conference of Ministers of Culture as one of the most serious obstacles to efficient planning:[9]

> In my opinion, the true reason for the deplorable conditions in West German education is the necessity to reach agreement (in the KMK) and hence "negative consensus"—along with the principle of strictly nonpublic sessions: one single Land can obstruct the common progress and common planning for all other Länder, and there is no effective political tool to prevent this.

Nationwide planning made some headway when Federal-State bodies were established since —unlike procedures of the Conference of Cultural Ministers—they do not require unanimous consensus. However, since the Bund does not rank above the Länder in the planning and decision-making processes of the Federal-State commissions, it cannot eliminate the systemwide planning problems. Hence, in 1977 the head of the department of higher education in the BMBW summed up the work of the Planning Committee as follows: "The way in which the common task is set up leaves little room for the Bund to do its own constructive planning. The Bund can at best suggest projects, but it cannot request them."[10] That is, the participation of the Bund is generally limited to joint decisions on the applications of individual Länder and perhaps to withhold its consent if it considers their success to be questionable. The Bund, however, is not in the position to effect special regional or academic schemes in accordance with its own ideas of comprehensive planning. For example, for a long time it has been necessary to increase study facilities for dentistry because there are clear indications that in this *numerus clausus* discipline future demand will far exceed the number of available places. The Länder, however, hesitate to submit development plans for this area because of the high costs for the establishment of dentistry facilities. Eberhard Böning has summarized the Bund's function in the Planning Committee as follows:[11]

> Practical experience has shown that the Bund can have a rather significant influence on the form of individual construction projects. It does, however, not play an essential part in comprehensive planning. This is, of course, quite the contrary of the original intention of the common task.

In general, it is evident that the Bund is dissatisfied with the powers and possibilities it has been given in the area of higher education. The Federal Minister of Education and Science has listed the most important aspects of the dissatisfaction in its Educational Policy Interim Report of 1976:[12]

— The change of the Basic Law in 1969 has resulted in a narrowly restricted participation of the Bund in higher education; yet the public holds it responsible for actual development to a far greater extent.
— From the point of view of the Bund, there are serious differences of opinion as to the required extent of joint planning and the binding force of joint resolutions. According to the various demarcation resolutions by the Länder (1972 and 1974), joint educational planning of the Bund and the Länder is to be limited to basic and rather abstract decisions. The Bund considers this a restriction of the cooperation suggested by constitutional law and a violation both of the exact terms and of the intent of the original agreement.

The report further points out that, in parliamentary debates, the governments apparently do not always use the joint planning decisions of the systemwide bodies as guidelines for their actions. Some Länder do not limit their expansionary efforts to those areas where deficiencies have been detected; rather, they attempt in some areas to exceed the planning targets established on the systemwide level. The report is also critical of the fact that up till now the Federal-State Commission could only submit nationwide inventories that are not structured according to Länder and regions. This makes it impossible to check whether the development of the educational system in the individual Länder conforms to the targets of the comprehensive educational plan.

The interim report of the Bund on the six-year cooperation with the Länder ends on a note of resignation. It toys with the idea of another, more effective, amendment to the Basic Law which would favor the Bund "if the Bund and the Länder, in their joint educational planning, should prove incapable of agreeing on the decisions that will be necessary for the educational system in the years to come."[13]

Also along this line is the policy declaration of the Federal Chancellor in December 1976 in which a "Report on the Structural Problems of the Federalist System of Education" that is to examine the distribution of competences between Bund and Länder was announced. Under the perspective of maintaining and promoting unity of living conditions in the Federal Republic this "Deficiency Report" by the Federal Government, to be published in February 1978, is not so much focused on problems of the higher education system but rather on divergent developments in the areas of secondary and vocational education and in teacher training. Yet it can be expected that the discussion of this report and the reaction of the Länder to it will once again bring into fore the basic problems of cooperation between Bund and Länder in education and indeed higher education policy.

Looking back on their cooperation hitherto it may be summarized that it was not so much based on a genuine wish for a constructive partnership, but rather was a partnership of expediency into which they had been forced by external circumstances. In this partnership, the Bund believes that it has too little authority to plan and decide, while the Länder see to it that there is not too much interference in their cultural autonomy.

This relationship between the Bund and the Länder does not come as a surprise if one considers the background against which the "common tasks" were formulated in 1969. At that time, the

Bavarian minister of culture warned the Bavarian parliament that the authority[14]

> for decisions in the area of educational and university planning is challenged and that the Bund is trying to monopolize it. . . . There is no need for the federal government to have authority in educational planning. . . . In their activities, the Länder are supported by the Science Council and the Education Council, both of which have been created jointly by the Bund and the Länder for this purpose. The federal government is sufficiently represented in both agencies to be able to attend to its own interests. If the federal government has failed to do so, it must blame itself, not the Länder.

In the same context, the government of Baden Württemberg, in anticipation of the "Deficiency Report" of the Federal Government, has just voiced its concern that positive competition between the Länder has been blocked and must be restored. The state government argues, for example, that the introduction of the common tasks into the Basic Law "did not stand the test and that these could have long ago been substituted by better forms of cooperation, if only the Länder would be financially equipped in line with their tasks."[15]

It is hard to foresee whether this new round in the controversy over the competences of Bund and Länder will result in revised arrangements. With certainty, however, planning and decision making with regard to higher education will remain a bone of contention between the Bund and the Länder for some time. It can only be hoped that the creative potential of the federal principle will outweigh the limited efficiency which is also connected with decentralization.

Relationship Between Government and Institutions

The 1971 OECD analysis of the German educational system criticized the excess of bureaucracy, centralization, and supervision by the state authorities with regard to the primary and secondary system of education.[16] In comparison, the universities traditionally had greater latitude for autonomy. However, because of the sometimes chaotic conditions at the universities, the excesses of the student movement, and the demand for new forms of university constitutions, the trend at universities, since the beginning of the 1970s, has been toward stronger governmental interference. This is reflected in the university laws of the Länder and in a wealth of regulations.

It must be said, though, that the resulting loss of autonomy concerns partly areas in which the universities themselves had been ineffective and which, for reasons of efficiency, the government now considers it necessary to take over. Partly it also has been forced to do so following decrees of the Federal Constitutional Court which has more and more often been appealed to, to settle conflicts in the higher education sector.

At present, the increasing "legalization" is an important characteristic for the changing relation between government and higher education. A positive aspect of this development may be seen in the fact that the legislative responsibility of parliaments is evoked in this sector in which administrative executive powers had prevailed in lieu of legal regulations. Critical, however, is the tendency to remit open issues of educational policy, disguised as law suits, to the courts, thus assigning to them an outstanding role in policymaking. Moreover, the increasing "legalization" runs the risk of generating a narrow web of rules and regulations detrimental to any academic creativity.

There is uncertainty over the course that changing relations between the government and the universities will take. This uncertainty sometimes leads to a surprising change of fronts. For instance, at the 1973 Conference of Rectors the rector of the very progressive university at Bremen demanded that the new responsibilities of the university be formulated as much as possible by the government. He believed that the function of the university had changed. The traditional university was an institution that had no social obligation, that defined itself tautologically, and that represented an ungoverned, immeasurable system:[17]

A change of such a tautologically defined, immeasurable system into an expedient and productive system must generate friction; it cannot go according to plan. This is the basis from which we must proceed. And it will probably take many years before we have reached our goal. This goal, which quite rightly is again and again advocated by the ministers of culture, is the change of the universities into expedient and productive organizations. It will involve a change of the entire university structure, and we cannot yet define what this structure is going to be because the criteria have not yet been determined and established. That cannot be done without damage.

One government representative, the rather conservative minister of culture of Rhineland Palatinate, who attended this meeting thought that such expectations of the government went too far. He preferred to leave some areas of autonomy to the universities and not to see them reduced to achievement-oriented productive enterprises for society. He also thought that the demand to make the government responsible for defining and executing the tasks of the universities was too extreme.[18]

The truth is that the relationship between the government and higher education has changed for the worse. The lines are primarily drawn between the institutions and the executive branch of government, while the legislative branch remains in the shadow of the executive. There are many points of friction and controversy: the development and outcomes of the Frame Law for Higher Education passed by the federal government, and its transformation into Länder laws (which is being implemented with varying degrees of rigidity); the methods used when the constitutional loyalty of academic personnel is examined; the procedures by which study regulations for all academic fields are approved; and the growing use of the government's power to interfere with appointments through ministers of culture, and so on.

Apart from these controversial areas, a certain clumsiness of the cultural government bureaucracy in its daily contact with the universities has also added to the deterioration of the general climate. Rectors, chancellors, and professors are constantly called into the state capitals for official meetings and other business in order to listen to the latest governmental decisions, but not, however, to discuss them in their own terms.

An especially drastic example of this occurred recently at the Ministry of Culture of Baden-Württemberg. In the week before the 1976/77 Christmas vacation, the minister of culture presented the rectors at a state conference with an envelope that contained, without any further explanations, the draft of an order to eliminate 1,390 positions at the institutions of higher education. In view of the fact that an excess of primary and secondary teachers was projected and there was a scarcity of funds, the government officials asked the universities to submit plans for cutbacks in departments educating school teachers. When the universities did not respond to this request, the Ministry of Culture drew up its own plan. Among other things, it provided for the dissolution by ministerial decree of no less than six departments at the University of Stuttgart and seven departments at the University of Mannheim.

Meanwhile, the cultural ministry of Baden-Württemberg has made an effort to improve cooperation in this matter. The plan for staff elimination was later integrated into a "Structural Plan for Higher Education" which also included considerations relating to future expansions in the higher education sector and this structural plan was discussed with the rectors.

Yet such incidents have an adverse impact on cooperative planning by government and higher education, in addition to the spontaneous reactions of protest evoked by the manner in which the government proceeds. As the University of Konstanz has commented:[19]

> Although this incident was later minimized as a mere "suggestion" and was subsequently retracted, it is still pending since it is to be implemented in stages. Above all, it still makes us wonder if educational planning by the government of Baden-Württemberg is really to be trusted; the present policy of cutting down personnel together with capacity regulations and their latent ideology of "efficiency," may also in other states *nolens volens* threaten to give the coup de grace to the stagnant university reform.

The danger of a government dictate in the present situation is very real. In the face of growing problems, the government and the public have become weary of ineffectual discussions conducted in universities. In this, one must not forget that the executive branch of government did not fall upon the academic bone like a starving dog that has just been unleashed. On the contrary, the dog has avoided this particularly indigestible meal as long as possible, and probably for too long. One should also remember that cultural government bureaucracies are themselves the advocates of higher education and that they consider it their job to create a flourishing system of higher education. In the sixties and seventies, competing with other sectors, cultural ministries have been able to allocate an above average proportion of the budgets to institutions of higher education which is an external sign of their support.

Government officials are definitely aware of the dilemma which has made them the antagonist of the universities. The head of the department of higher education at the BMBW pictures the cultural official as moving confusedly over the battlefield between government and university:[20]

> Whether he wants to or not, he must participate in combat, although he also ought to act as a medic; he is to supply the politicians with ammunition and to dress the wounds of the academics. He is the one who personifies government actions.

The official also criticized the general animosity toward the government bureaucracy and the frequent attacks on officials; yet he believed that this bureaucracy could do with some self-criticism:[21]

> If the laws are to be carried out properly, if civil rights are to be implemented, and if public services are to be well administered, bureaucracy as such is inevitable and indispensible. But the kind of bureaucracy that is currently developing has a deadly effect on creative thinking, on flexibility, and on the imagination. However, we need all this to solve the problems of the next decade which affects the life of those children who were born in the years of a high birth rate; hence, in my opinion, it is a matter of maintain-

ing our social and political peace. The protest movement directed against bureaucratization is to be taken very seriously. The solidarity of the citizens in the academic sector against government bureaucracy threatens to become a solidarity against the government.

This pessimistic prognosis should not be ignored, in view of increased discussion relating to a general dissatisfaction with government in the Federal Republic and of the number of documents that reveal the negative attitude of university professors toward the cultural government bureaucracy.

According to a poll of university professors in the 1976/77 winter semester, two-thirds of the professors consider "the freedom of research and teaching imperiled by increasing government regimentation." More than half of them (56 percent) denied that universities today require "government help and intervention to be able to carry out their responsibilities at all."[22] Another poll of university professors, conducted at the same time, confirms the troubled relations between the government and universities. No more than 17 percent of the professors described relations between the Ministry of Culture and academics as "relatively cooperative," while 54 percent considered them "rather tense."[23]

The chairman of the Science Council from 1972–1976 made some pertinent comments when he looked back upon his term in office. He pointed to the politicizing of internal university discussions as a reason for the shift of the scales of power in favor of the ministries of culture. The shift is apparent in the novation of the laws for higher education that are presently discussed by the Länder.[24]

> Internal university controversies about goals, programs, and hiring procedures generally involve all areas of self-government. The more political these controversies become, the less room there is for consensus and thus for self-government; hence, the sphere of government influence becomes broader; it extends even to those traditionally autonomous areas that concern the organization of teaching and the selection of research subjects; and as a consequence, the

appointment proposals become less obligatory for the government.

At the same time, the former chairman emphasized the fact that the universities have not met their responsibilities in the face of changing demands:[25]

> If, however, there is a discrepancy between the responsibilities a university believes it has, and the demand put upon it by the public, a conflict between the state and the university must necessarily arise. The number of government regulations rises. . . . The growing self-confidence of the government is based on older German traditions. It is therefore no surprise if the government fills the void that has been created by internal conflicts and the inadequate awareness of future needs.

The former chairman of the Science Council hopes that in the future the institutions of higher education, especially the universities, will consider it their duty to find a new consensus, so that they may once again regain autonomy. He asks the government not to exploit present weaknesses at the institutions to such an extent that their long-term vitality is impaired.[26]

To sum up, we may say that the relationship between the Bund and the Länder, and between the government and higher education in the Federal Republic, is a preeminent example of the complexity of the question asking for the efficiency of centralized and decentralized factors in a system of higher education. In the past, the lack of systemwide planning on one side was matched by the principle of university autonomy on the other, even though these had always been government institutions.

In the new moves toward a "cooperative federalism" the Länder lose some of their powers to the higher level of federal planning. Simultaneously, on the lower level they strengthen their influence over the institutions of higher education and, by this, elicit a negative reaction from those institutions. It seems to us that the future efficiency of the system of higher education in the Federal Republic of Germany will largely depend on the way in which the sensitive balance between autonomy and centralized planning will be maintained. There is not much cause for optimism since this precarious process takes place at a time when distrust and disputes about competence dominate—rather than a climate of constructive cooperation between the three levels of the Bund, the Länder, and the institutions of higher education.

FOOTNOTES

1. For example, the Federal-State Commission formed in June 1970 listed several hundred meetings of all the committees until the so-called "priority paper" was issued in the summer of 1972. In February 1974 alone sixteen committee meetings of the Federal-State Commission took place. Cf. Eberhard Böning, "Bildungsgesamtplan—eine Gleichung nur mit Unbekannten?" *Frankfurter Rundschau* (June 15, 1974).
2. Hildegard Hamm-Brücher, *Unfähig zur Reform?* Kritik und Initiativen zur Bildungsreform (München: Piper, 1972), pp. 38–39. From 1967–1969, Hildegard Hamm-Brücher was undersecretary in Hesse and therefore participated in the meetings of the KMK. From 1969–1972 she was undersecretary in the BMBW and was an ex officio member of almost all important committees for educational policy.
3. Cf. the "Hasemann-Papier"—geheime Skizze über neue Struktur des Planungswesens in der Bildungspolitik, *Input*, I (1971), pp. 30–31.
4. Many of the Länder ministers also would prefer an integration of the work of the Planning Commission and the BLK "so that we can at least dispose of one of our many duties." (Minister of Culture Vogel—Rhineland Palatinate). Cf. West German Conference of University Rectors, *Was erwartet der Staat von der Mitwirkung der Hochschulen?*, Jahresversammlung 1973, Dokumente zur Hochschulreform XXII/1973 (Bonn-Bad Godesberg: 1973), p. 29.
5. "Hasemann-Papier," *op. cit.*, p. 32.
6. West German Conference of Rectors, *Qualität und Quantität—Die Hochschule im Schatten des Studentenberges*, Jahresversammlung 1976, Dokumente zur Hochschulreform XXX/1976 (Bonn-Bad Godesberg: 1977), p. 25.
7. Hildegard Hamm-Brücher, *op. cit.*, p. 8.
8. *Ibid.*, p. 40.
9. *Ibid.*, p. 20.

10. Eberhard Böning, "Hochschulrahmenplanung," Deutsch-amerikanische Tagung über Rechtsprobleme des Hochschulrahmenzugangs, March, 1977 (manuscript), p. 23. (To be published 1978 in the journal *Wissenschaftsrecht, Wissenschaftsverwaltung, Wissenschaftsförderung*).
11. *Ibid.*, p. 24.
12. Cf. Federal Ministry for Education and Science, *Bildungspolitische Zwischenbilanz* (Bonn: 1976), pp. 82–83.
13. *Ibid.*, p. 87.
14. Ludwig Huber, *Schul- und Hochschulreform*, Speech on the budget by the Bavarian minister of education and culture in the Bavarian Parliament on March 12, 1969, p. 26.
15. State Ministry of Baden Württemberg, "Die Vorteile des Föderalismus in der Kulturpolitik I." (Stuttgart 2.1. 1978 p. 11 (mimeo).
16. OECD, Reviews of National Policies for Education: Germany. Paris, 1972, pp. 105–6.
17. West German Conference of Rectors (Annual Meeting 1973), *op. cit.*, p. 88 (van der Vring, Rector of the University of Bremen).
18. *Ibid.*, p. 105 (Vogel, minister of culture of Rhineland Palatinate).
19. Hans Robert Jaus and Herbert Nesselhauf, eds., *Gebremste Reform*, Ein Kapitel deutscher Hochschulgeschichte, Universität Konstanz 1966–1976 (Konstanz: Universitätsverlag, 1977), p. XIV.
20. Eberhard Böning, "Der Wissenschaftsbeamte–zu den Versuchen der Bürokratisierung der Wissenschaft," *Die Deutsche Universitätszeitung* (1977), p. 470.
21. *Ibid.*, p. 475.
22. Cf. Infratest Sozialforschung, *Befragung des Wissenschaftlichen Personals der Hochschulen zur Fortentwicklung von Lehre und Forschung*, Winter Semester 1976/77 (Munich: 1977), p. 364.
23. Institut für Demoskopie Allensbach, *Die Lage der Forschung an den Deutschen Universitäten*, Erster Bericht über eine Repräsentativbefragung (Allensbach: 1977), p. 11.
24. Theodor Heidhues, "Bericht des Vorsitzenden des Wissenschaftsrates of January 23, 1976," in Science Council, *Empfehlungen und Stellungnahmen 1975*, pp. 298–99.
25. *Ibid.*, pp. 299–300.
26. Cf. *ibid.*, pp. 300–1.

APPENDIX

APPENDIX A

TABLE A1
Data for Gross National Product, Public Expenditure, Educational Budget
and Expenditure on Higher Education

Year	GNP Billion DM	Index	Public Expenditure Billion DM	Index	Educational Budget Billion DM	Index	Expenditure on Higher Education Billion DM	Index
	(1)	(2)	(3)	(4)	(5)	(6)	(7)	(8)
1961	332.6	100	95.3	100	9.0	100	1.7	100
1962	360.1	108	107.2	113	10.2	113	2.1	124
1963	384.0	116	117.1	123	11.7	130	2.4	141
1964	420.9	127	128.1	157	13.8	153	2.9	171
1965	460.4	138	139.2	171	15.7	174	3.5	206
1966	490.7	148	145.1	178	17.0	189	3.7	218
1967	495.5	149	153.8	189	17.8	198	4.0	235
1968	540.0	162	158.8	195	19.1	212	4.4	259
1969	605.2	182	174.3	214	22.2	247	5.3	312
1970	685.6	206	196.3	241	27.6	307	6.9	406
1971	761.9	229	226.8	279	34.7	386	8.4	494
1972	833.9	251	252.1	310	39.1	434	9.4	553
1973	926.9	279	280.1	344	44.5	494	10.7	629
1974	995.7	299	315.0	387	52.6	584	12.8	753
1975	1,040.4	313	361.0	444	56.2	624	13.5	794

Source:
Column (1): 1961–64: Statistisches Jahrbuch für die Bundesrepublik Deutschland (Stuttgart: Kohlhammer, 1976), p. 516.
1965–75: BMBW, Grund- und Strukturdaten, 1976 (Bonn: 1976), p. 131.
Column (3): 1961–64: Statistisches Jahrbuch, *ibid.*, p. 403.
1965–75: BMBW, *ibid.*, p. 131.
Column (5): 1961–64: Statistisches Jahrbuch, *ibid.*, p. 403.
1965–75: BMBW, *ibid.*, p. 122.
Column (7): 1961–64: Willi Albert, Christoph Oehler, Materialien zur Entwicklung der Hochschulen 1950–67 (HIS-Hochschulforschung, Bd. 1) (Hannover: 1969), p. 351.
1964–75: BMBW, *ibid.*, p. 122.

TABLE A2
Breakdown of Educational Budget*

Educational Budget, 1975[1]	Billion DM	Contribution of the Bund in %
Elementary Sector, Extracurricular Youth Education	2.0	6.1
Schools (primary and secondary level)	33.2	0.3
Higher Education[2]	13.5	10.5
Further Education[3]	1.3	10.4
Other sectors of Education	4.0	49.0
General Research Promotion	2.1	45.9
Total	56.2	8.4

* This table shows the breakdown of the "Educational Budget" of Column 5 in Table A1 (expenditure on education and research as defined in the comprehensive educational plan of the Federal-State Commission). Total expenditure for education and science in a broader sense was 870 billion DM in 1975. In addition to the educational budget this includes also the following: big science and departmental research, including defense research (7.0 billion DM); measures of the Bundesanstalt für Arbeit (3.3 billion DM); and, on the part of the private economic sector, expenditure for vocational training (10.0 billion DM) and for research and development (10.5 billion DM). (cf. BMBW, Grund- und Strukturdaten, 1976, S. 120).

1. cf. BMBW, Grund- und Strukturdaten, 1976 (Bonn: 1976), p. 120 and 125 and BMBW, Bildung im Zahlenspiegel, edition 1975 (Stuttgart: 1976), p. 207.
2. Vocational training, promotion of civil education, public libraries, adult education.
3. Including financial aid to students in secondary and higher education and continuing education for teachers.

SELECTED BIBLIOGRAPHY

(References on German higher education in English)

Böning, E., K. Roeloffs, *Three German Universities—Aachen, Bochum, Konstanz. Case Studies on Innovation in Higher Education.* OECD. Paris, 1970.

Burn, B., *Higher Education in Nine Countries,* New York: McGraw-Hill, 1977.

Cathy, G., G. Drilhon, et al., *The Research System.* Comparative Survey of the Organization and Financing of Fundamental Research. Vol. I: France, Germany, United Kingdom. OECD. Paris, 1972.

Framhein, G., H. Peisert, "Graduates' Views on Higher Education," in A. Bonboir, ed., *Instructional Design in Higher Education—Innovation in Curricula and Teaching.* Proceedings of the 2nd Congress of the European Association for Research and Development in Higher Education. Louvain-la-Neuve, 1976.

Geimer, R., H. Geimer, in cooperation with U. Schmidt, *Science in the Federal Republic of Germany.* Organization and Promotion. Published by the German Academic Exchange Service, Bonn-Bad Godesberg, 1978 (4th edition).

Goldschmidt, D., S. Hübner, "Changing Concepts of the University in Society: The West German Case," in *Higher Education in a Changing World.* World Yearbook 1971/72. Brian Holmes and David C. Scanlon, eds., London: Evans, 1971.

Goldschmidt, D., "West Germany," in M. Scotford Archer, ed., *Students, University, and Society.* London: Heinemann, 1972.

Goldschmidt, D., "Autonomy and Accountability of Higher Education in the Federal Republic of Germany," in P. G. Altbach, ed., *The University's Response to Societal Demands.* ICED. New York, 1975.

Van de Graaff, J., Burton Clark, et al., *Academic Power: Patterns of Authority,* New York: Praeger, 1978.

Huber, L., "Developments in Higher Education in Europe: Background Report, German Speaking Countries." Council of Europe, *Strategies for Research and Development in Higher Education.* Noel Entwistle, ed., Amsterdam: Swets and Zeitlinger, 1976.

OECD, *Reviews of National Policies for Education: Germany.* Paris, 1972.

Teichler, U., "Problems of West German Universities on the Way to Mass Higher Education," *Western European Education*, Vol. VIII, No. 1–2, 1976.

DIRECTORS OF COUNTRY STUDIES

Australia
Bruce Williams, Vice-Chancellor and Principal, University of Sydney.
Canada
Edward Sheffield, Professor of Higher Education, Chairman, Higher Education Group, University of Toronto.
Sponsor: Higher Education Group, University of Toronto.
Federal Republic of Germany
Hansgert Peisert, Professor, Zentrum I, Bildungsforschung, University of Konstanz.
Sponsor: University of Konstanz.
France
Alain Binenaymé, Professor of Economics, University of Paris-Dauphine IX.
Sponsor: Secretary of State for Higher Education.
Iran
Abdol Hossein Samii, Director, Imperial Medical Center of Iran.
M. Reza Vaghefi, Dean, School of Economics, University of Tehran.
Sponsor: Reza Shah Kabir University.
Japan
Katsuya Narita, Director of First Research Department, National Institute for Educational Research.
Sponsor: National Institute for Educational Research.
Mexico
Alfonso Rangel Guerra, General Director of Higher Education, Secretaría de Educación Publica.

Sponsor: Asociación Nacional de Universidades e Institutos de Enseñanza Superior.

Poland
Jan Szczepański, Professor, Instiute of Philosophy, Warsaw.
Sponsor Institute for Higher Education Research.

Sweden
Bertil Östergren, Adviser, National Board of Universities and Colleges.
Sponsor: National Board of Universities and Colleges.

Thailand
Sippanondha Ketudat, Secretary-General, National Education Commission.
Sponsor: National Education Commission.

United Kingdom
Anthony Becher, Professor of Education, University of Sussex.
Jack Embling, Former Deputy Under Secretary of State, Department of Education and Science.
Maurice Kogan, Professor of Government and Social Administration, Brunel University.
Sponsor: Leverhulme Trust.

United States
John R. Shea, Carnegie Council for Policy Studies in Higher Education.
David D. Henry, President Emeritus, University of Illinois at Urbana-Champaign.
Lyman A. Glenny, Center for Research and Development in Higher Education, University of California, Berkeley.
Sponsor: International Council for Educational Development.